# INTRODUCTION
## to the
# SEVEN RAYS

by

**KURT ABRAHAM**

**LAMPUS PRESS
19211 ANTIOCH ROAD
WHITE CITY, OREGON 97503**

Dedicated to

BOB and NANCY BATEN
and
JOHN BERGES

## ACKNOWLEDGEMENTS

For permission to use copyright material the author gratefully acknowledges the following:

The Lucis Trust for permission to quote from Alice Bailey's *Esoteric Psychology, Destiny of Nations, Discipleship in the New Age, Telepathy and the Etheric Vehicle,* and *Problems of Humanity.*

BOOKS BY KURT ABRAHAM

Psychological Types and the Seven Rays (1983)

Threefold Method for Understanding the Seven Rays
and Other Essays in Esoteric Psychology (1984)

Introduction to the Seven Rays (1986)

The Seven Rays and Nations:
France and the United States Compared (1987)

The Moon Veils Vulcan and the Sun Veils Neptune (1989)

Balancing the Pairs of Opposites; The Seven Rays and Education,
and Other Essays in Esoteric Psychology (1993)

Techniques of Soul Alignment; The Rays, the Subtle Bodies, and
the Use of Keywords (1997)

# CONTENTS

# THE QUALIFYING TERMS OF THE SEVEN RAYS

There is the need to introduce the Seven Rays in such a way as to make it accessible to more people. At the same time there is also a great need to minimize the distortion that tends to occur in the stepping down process so that the integrity of the subject matter is maintained.

Beginning with a definition: "A ray is but a name for a particular force or type of energy, with the emphasis upon the quality which that force exhibits and not upon the form aspect which it creates" (*Esoteric Psychology*, v. 1, p. 316).

What does it mean to emphasize *quality* rather than *form*? Consider the following correspondences of the three basic aspects:

| Life | Quality | Appearance |
|------|---------|------------|
| Spirit | Consciousness | Form |
| Monad | Soul | Personality |
| Purpose | Love | Activity |
| Will | Wisdom | Intelligence |

At first glance it may seem next to impossible to know anything in a concrete sense about such relative abstractions as "quality", "consciousness" or "soul." Indeed, one's attention is continually drawn to the world of "form", "activity" and "appearances" to the point that anything less concrete is viewed skeptically and dubiously. The supposition here, however, is that the world of appearances is actually brought into being by the qualitative world. The world of form is an expression of the "inner" worlds of quality, soul, and spirit. The issuing forth of new life-forms is a result of the consciousness-quality of soul and the will-purpose of spirit. This is our supposition. It is a supposition upon which the study of the seven ray energies sheds considerable light.

1

In our exploration two modes of thought are required. We could call these modes of thought the scientific mode and the "religious" or spiritual mode. The *scientific mode* requires above all *clear thinking*, the ability to make *clear differentiation between what is known and what is hypothetical*. The scientific mode also requires the power to make *detached observations*, including observations of very subtle psychological states and processes. The scientific mode of thought need not at all be limited to gross physical plane phenomena in order for it to be scientific.

The *"religious" mode* of thought has nothing to do with religious doctrine or dogma. Religious thought looks in a spiritual direction and seeks *inspiration, illumination, and intuition*. Scientific thought relies on its own innate power of reason and observation. Religious-spiritual thought recognizes the limitations of one's own reasoning abilities and seeks to align itself with the trans-personal source. In other words, to put it very succinctly, both the *heart* (the quality of love) and the *head* (the quality of intelligence) are needed in this scientific approach into the worlds of quality and consciousness.

**The Seven Rays Energies—Their Qualifying Names**. As mentioned in the book Esoteric Psychology, "There is nothing in the whole solar system, at whatever stage of evolution it may stand, which does not belong and has not always belonged to one or another of the seven rays."

The names of the seven rays are listed below. These identifying terms call our attention to the qualitative world rather than to the world of appearance-form.

I. Ray of Will or Power
II. Ray of Love-Wisdom
III. Ray of Intelligent Activity or Adaptability
IV. Ray of Harmony through Conflict, also called the
   Ray of Beauty and Art
V. Ray of Scientific Knowledge
VI. Ray of Idealism and Devotion
VII Ray of Organization, also known as the
   Ray of Ceremonial Magic

**The Rays and the Seven Planes of the Solar System.** All the rays manifest on all seven planes of the solar system, but certain rays tend to rule or dominate on a particular plane. Each plane is divided into seven sub-planes, which would make a total of 49 sub-planes. We are familiar with some of the sub-planes of the physical plane. The seven sub-planes of the physical plane, moving from the most refined to the densest are:

1. first ether
2. second ether
3. third ether
4. fourth ether
5. gaseous sub-plane
6. liquid
7. solid

It can be noted that magnetism and electricity are phenomena of the etheric sub-planes. Magnetism is something that is neither solid, liquid, nor gas. One cannot see magnetism with normal sight. One can, however, readily detect its presence. One can see its effects.

The major planes and their rays are indicated below:

| Plane | Ray |
|---|---|
| 1. Plane of Adi or Divinity.... | Ray I.....Will, Power |
| 2. Plane of the Monad ........ | Ray II....Love-Wisdom |
| 3. Plane of Atma or Spirit.... | Ray III...Active Intelligence |
| 4. Plane of Buddhi, Intuition | Ray IV...Harmony, Beauty |
| 5. Mental Plane (Manas)..... | Ray V....Concrete Knowledge |
| 6. Emotional Plane (Astral). | Ray VI...Idealism, Devotion |
| 7. Physical Plane.............. | Ray VII...Organization |

There is an interesting correspondence between the 6th sub-plane of the physical plane (liquid sub-plane), the 6th major plane (or plane of emotion, sentience), and the 6th ray of idealism and devotion.

Throughout the solar system there is a complex interweaving of the seven rays energies that cannot be comprehended by the human intellect. The question then becomes: Where and how to begin a study of the subtle energies of the seven rays? It is necessary to proceed to a point and level where we can recognize in some immediately discernable way the presence of the ray energies. It is necessary to step out of the hypothetical and into the observable. The answer to the question above becomes then: *One begins with a study of the human being—with the psychological make-up of a human being.* To understand the energy of consciousness and quality, it is necessary to begin with ourselves.

At the outset it is necessary to emphasize that we are not being asked to accept anything blindly or on faith alone. Everything here is presented in a hypothetical way only. All of us will "test" the knowledge or the hypotheses in the light of our own experience. We ask only that the reader keep an open mind, and a listening heart.

**The Most Important Key to Understanding the Seven Rays in the Psychological Make-Up of a Human Being**. There is a most direct correlation between the first three rays (the rays of aspect) and the Trinity (which can be found in many major religions under various names). Will, Love, and Light (or Purpose, Wisdom and Intelligence) are qualities of Deity (or ray energies) that have been anthropomorphized in various religions down the ages. These truths have long been given out in a variety of forms and in a variety of Teachings. The qualities and significance of the seven—the septenate—however has just recently been given out to the wider, exoteric audience. Along with the *three rays of aspect* (the basic Trinity), the septenate also includes *the four rays of attribute*.

The lower three (or the downward pointing triangle) is related to the Trinity, or the upward pointing triangle, with the bridging or synthesizing ray represented as the point in the center.

The question once again quickly becomes: How can these apparent abstraction or hypotheses be brought to a place of observation and then knowing, particularly in terms of human psychology? The following key is extremely helpful in the answering of that question:

*The Soul* ..........................can be on any one of the seven rays.
(Not all soul types, however, are in incarnation at any given time.)

    *The Personality* ........can also on any one of the seven rays.
    (The personality is, in a sense, a sub-ray of the causal
    and dominant soul ray.)

        The Mind...................generally on either ray 1, 4, or 5
        Emotional Body.........generally on ray 2 or 6
        Physical Body............generally on ray 3 or 7

This paradigm is of considerable help in understanding the ray energies, as they energize and condition the life of an individual human being. At this point we could say that there are up to five rays that play through the life of an individual (not including the ray of the monad or spirit). One or two of the rays will be more dominant than others. The soul ray may not be evident in the relatively undeveloped person. During different stages of development a particular "body" and ray will receive the focus of energy. For example, during the 14-21 year old cycle (and also the 21-25 year cycle) the ray of the mental body will very likely be central.

It is necessary to emphasize, however, that every person is unique. No two people are alike. Yet similarities abound. One could say that 50% of the people in the world are women. That does not mean that 50% of the people are identical. Yet there are patterns and there are similarities. The seven rays hold the key to the mystery of psychological type—a mystery that science has hardly been able to approach, let alone solve. The seven rays hold also one of the keys to the mystery of level of manifestation. These two most subtle phenomena—*type and level*—is the subject matter of our esoteric psychological exploration.

**The First Ray of Will and Purpose**. This energy gives rise to the *power type*: the king, the ruler, the governor, the statesman, the president, the manager, the administrator, the law-enforcer, the leader.

Some of the qualities of this type include a sense of understanding of issues that relate to power, a managerial or administrative ability, skill in handling people, a sense of strength and responsibility, persistence and steadfastness, and a sense of justice. Some of the worst examples of this type would be the ruthless tyrants, the despot, the dictator. Some of the negative characteristics of this type would be cruelty, total disregard for the feelings of others, personal ambition, ruthlessness, destructiveness, and the will to personal power. Some of the better examples of this type would include the benevolent dictator, the diplomatic statesman, the concerned administrator, and the responsible leader with a true vision of right direction.

Power in a certain sense is responsibility over some aspect of the lives of others. The power figure contributes to the formulation of laws, policies, rules and regulations, or is instrumental in carrying out laws and policies, in order to bring order to the collective life. The first ray type must necessarily have a wide overview of the collective unit (the business, the organization, community, etc.) and must also be in touch with all departments or subsidiary units. This type, however, tends not to have detailed knowledge of, say, a subsidiary department in the way that a scientific type would have. The 5th ray scientific type would tend to master a field of knowledge; the 1st ray power type would be aware of all power issues in an organization—a far different quality.

To quote from Alice Bailey's *Esoteric Psychology*, v. 1, p.201: "This has been spoken of as the ray of power, and it is correctly so called, but if it were power alone, without wisdom and love, a destructive and disintegrating force would result. When however, the three characteristics are united, it becomes a creative and governing ray. Those on this ray have strong will power, for either good or evil, for the former when the will is directed by wisdom and made selfless by love. The first ray man will always 'come to the front' in his own line. He may be the burglar or the judge who condemns him, but in either case he will be at the head of his profession. He is the born leader in any and every public career, one to trust and lean on, one to defend the weak and put down oppression, fearless of consequences and

6

utterly indifferent to comment. On the other hand, an unmodified first ray can produce a man of unrelenting cruelty and hardness of nature."

**The Second Ray of Love-Wisdom.** This energy gives rise to the "love type, full of love and fusing power" (*Eso. Psych.*, v.1, p. 329). This type, from an archetypal point of view, is the wise counselor to the ruler and is generally attracted to religious or spiritual endeavors or wisdom teachings of some sort. Interested in the field of consciousness, this type will often make a good psychologist, counselor, or teacher. It should be remembered that one can teach and counselor through a great variety of means and forms. Some qualities evidenced by this type are patience, love, sympathy, wisdom, understanding, inclusiveness, teaching ability, a broad inclusive type of knowledge, healing or therapeutic ability, and a desire for peace, calmness, and unification. Some negative characteristics of the second ray type are lack of energy, a desire for personal popularity or the liking of being liked, over absorption in study, a longing for material security, fearfulness, over attachment, hypersensitivity, and a tendency to be overly protective.

Love and wisdom go hand in hand as do will and power. Love tends to bring about an appreciation and understanding of that which is other than oneself. Understanding and appreciation of "the other" help to bring about right relationship and a sense of unity. Wisdom is defined as "abilities to discern inner qualities and relationships, insight," "accumulated philosophical learning," and "good sense, judgment."

Wisdom, then, is a kind of knowing that goes deeper than an academic acquaintance with the form of things. It implies knowledge plus the seasoning that comes about through long and often difficult experiences. It implies familiarity with the form plus being en rapport with the being of another. As well as a form-to-form relationship, there is a soul-to-soul connection.

A negative trait of this contemplative type is over-absorption in study. In some cases this can lead to a failure to assume right responsibility. Responsibility, at one level, deals with tending to physical plane necessities. Interests in the more abstract planes of quality and consciousness can lead at time to a neglect of the physical plane necessities.

The ray energies generally manifest in combination with other rays. The softer, more sensitive qualities of the second ray prevent the first ray from becoming too destructive or cruel. The second ray brings wisdom to the scientific fifth ray and prevents the scientist from crystallizing or hardening into materialism. The second ray helps to tame some of the eccentricities of the fourth ray artistic type. The second ray of love helps the seventh ray of organization become a healer.

To quote from *Esoteric Psychology*: "This is called the ray of wisdom from its characteristic desire for pure knowledge and for absolute truth—cold and selfish, if without love, and inactive without power. When both power and love are present, then you have the ray of the Buddhas and of all great teachers of humanity,—those who, having attained wisdom for the sake of others, spend themselves in giving it forth. The student on this ray is ever unsatisfied with his highest attainments; no matter how great his knowledge, his mind is still fixed on the unknown, the beyond, and on the heights as yet unscaled.

"The second ray man will have tact and foresight; he will make an excellent ambassador, and a first-rate teacher or head of a college; as a man of affairs, he will have clear intelligence and wisdom in dealing with matters which come before him, and he will have the capacity of impressing true views of things on others and of making them see things as he does. He will make a good business man, if modified by the fourth, fifth and seventh rays. The soldier on this ray would plan wisely and foresee possibilities; he would have an intuition as to the best course to pursue, and he would never lead his men into danger through rashness. He might be deficient in rapidity of action and energy. The artist on this ray would always seek to teach through his art, and his pictures would have a meaning. His literary work would always be instructive" (vol. 1, p. 203).

**Third Ray of Active Intelligence**. This ray gives rise to the "active type, full of action and manipulating energy" (*Eso.*

*Psych.* v.1, 329). We come now to the third aspect of the triplicity Will-Love-Action or Spirit-Consciousness-Form. The Totality, symbolized by a Circle, has been divided into a Triplicty (the Trinity), symbolized by a Triangle within the Circle.

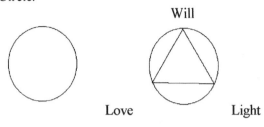

The Totality is greater than the sum of its parts. The third aspect is in a sense more "visible" than the first and second aspects in the same way that activity is more apparent than will or love, and behavior is more apparent than intent or feeling. Intelligence is more recognizable (more measurable) than purpose or wisdom.

The third ray of intelligent activity is often present in the businessman, the active man-of-affairs, the financier. This ray type can also be found in the field of education. It can also be the type of philosopher that employs primarily *reason*. With the third ray type, we generally find a very *energetic* person with a sharp and *quick intellect*. *Adaptability* is a key quality of the third ray type and is exemplified in the business man who constantly has to be making adaptations to meet the changing whims and demands of the market place. Another important quality is *planning*. The third ray type is a strategist—*scheming, planning ahead, manipulating*. There is often also a special ability to use words, the ability to find the most appropriate word, evidenced in *verbal and/or written skills*. An example could be the especially *articulate* university professor, or the salesman who is never at a loss for words.

Some negative characteristics of this type would include a busy-ness or hyperactivity, being constantly in motion but producing little lasting or significant results. Other negative characteristics include selfish manipulation through the use of the false word, an ability to deceive, excessive intellectualism, criticism and materialistic attitudes.

"This is the ray of the abstract thinker, of the philosopher and the metaphysician, of the man who delights in the higher mathematics but who, unless modified by some practical ray, would hardly be troubled to keep his accounts accurately. His imaginative faculty will be highly developed, i.e., he can by the power of his imagination grasp the essence of a truth; his idealism will often be strong; he is a dreamer and a theorist, and from his wide views and great caution he sees every side of a question equally clearly. This sometimes paralyses his action. He will make a good business man; as a soldier he will work out a problem in tactics at his desk, but is seldom great in the field. As an artist his technique is not fine, but his subjects will be full of thought and interest. He will love music, but unless influenced by the fourth ray he will not produce it. In all walks of life he is full of ideas, but is too impractical to carry them out.

"One type of this ray is unconventional to a degree, slovenly, unpunctual and idle, and regardless of appearances. If influenced by the fifth ray as the secondary ray this character is, entirely changed. The third and the fifth rays make the perfectly balanced historian who grasps his subject in a large way and verifies every detail with patient accuracy. Again the third and the fifth rays together make the truly great mathematician who soars into heights of abstract thought and calculation, and who can also bring his results down to practical scientific use. The literary style of the third ray man is too often vague and involved, but if influenced by the first, fourth, fifth or seventh rays, this is changed, and under the fifth he will be a master of the pen.

"The curing of disease by the third ray man would be by the use of drugs made of herbs or minerals belonging to the same ray as the patient whom he desires to relieve.

"The method of approaching the great Quest, for this ray type, is by deep thinking on philosophic or metaphysical lines till he is led to the realization of the great Beyond and of the paramount importance of treading the Path that leads thither." (*Esoteric Psychology*, vol. 1, pp. 204-5.)

10

**The Fourth Ray of Harmony Through Conflict**. This energy produces the "artistic type, full of a sense of beauty and creative aspiration" (*Esoteric Psychology*, v. i, p. 329).

The first three rays are know as the *rays of aspect*; the next four rays are know as the *rays of attribute*. Some of the qualities associated with the fourth ray type include creativity, creative imagination, intuition, sensitivity to beauty, refined sense of color, poetic faculty, ability to relieve tension through the use of humor, and, eventually, harmony, unity, and serenity.

Some of the negative characteristics include mood swings, fluctuations between hyperactivity and lethargy, manic or ecstatic states, followed by mild depression and withdrawal. Other problematical characteristics include unnecessary conflicts, exaggerations, and inaccuracy.

In the number "three" we have the unity and strength of the blended energies of the triangle. We have the trinity, the divine pattern, the transcendent and unmanifested. Something new transpires with the number "four." Here we find the corner stone and the building block, and we also find the conflicts and woes that go into the manifesting and creative endeavor.

The fourth ray has been called "the Lower than the Three, the Highest of the Four." It holds a mediating position between the higher and the lower, the formless and the form, the abstract and the concrete. It is bound to form, to the manifesting, but it endeavors to create the subtlest, most refined, most inspiring, most beautiful forms.

This is the artistic and creative faculty, but it may be expressed in creative life-styles and creative relationships, as well as in creative works of art. Manifestation, the building block, the square, the 90° angle are filled with conflict, with opposition, with cross purposes. The goal, however, is harmony, beauty and unity. This type often seeks to intuit the divine pattern, to sense the vision, and to seek inspiration. The effort to create a suitable outer form for the sensed inner vision can lead to difficulty and conflict.

"This has been called the 'ray of struggle' for on this ray the qualities of rajas (activity) and tamas (inertia) are so strangely equal in proportion that the nature of the fourth ray man is torn with their combat, and the outcome, when satisfactory, is spoken of as the 'Birth of Horus,' of the Christ, born from the throes of constant pain and suffering.

"Tamas induces love of ease and pleasure, a hatred of causing pain amounting to moral cowardice, indolence, procrastination, a desire to let things be, to rest, and to take no thought of the morrow. Rajas is fiery, impatient, ever urging to action. These contrasting forces in the nature make life one perpetual warfare and unrest for the fourth ray man; the friction and the experience gained thereby may produce very rapid evolution, but the man may as easily become a ne'er-do-well as a hero.

It is the ray of the dashing cavalry leader, reckless of risks to himself or his followers. It is the ray of the man who will lead a forlorn hope, for in moments of excitement the fourth ray man is entirely dominated by rajas; of the wild speculator and gambler, full of enthusiasm and plans, easily overwhelmed by sorrow or failure, but as quickly recovering from all reverses and misfortunes." *Esoteric Psychology*, v. i, p. 206.

**The Fifth Ray of Scientific Knowledge**. This energy gives rise to the "scientific type, full of the idea of cause and results. The mathematical type" (*Esoteric Psychology*, v. i, p. 329).

The fifth ray type is concerned with "concrete knowledge", as opposed to subtle or abstract knowledge. Concrete knowledge is concerned with the form of things, with the measurable and the provable. Whereas the artistic type tends to be concerned with a subjective experience, the scientific type is concerned with objective knowledge. The artistic type is concerned with creativity, with subtlety of feeling, and with self-expression. The scientific type is not concerned with creativity, but with *what is*. The scientist is concerned with *form*, not feeling, and with *detached observation*, not with self-expression.

Certainty of knowledge for this type is an end in itself. This type seeks to master a field of knowledge. Knowledge for a third ray type (intelligent activity) leads to activity, or is a means to an end, or is something that results in a practical enterprise. With the scientific type there is greater purity of knowledge, greater depth of knowledge, greater certainty, greater knowledge for the sake of knowledge. This type is less eager to seek practical application and more eager to probe deeper into what it is that is actually known.

The pure fifth ray type (if there is such a person) is free of any political agenda. Political agenda may further a political cause, but generally does not further knowledge.

The mental plane is conditioned and "ruled" by the fifth ray of science. The scientific thinker moves with ease on the mental plane. This is a plane of detachment. On the watery plane of emotional, one feels with or empathizes with something or someone, and to some degree one becomes a part of the other, psychologically speaking. On the mental plane one is able to remove oneself, to detach oneself, and observe. On the mental plane one can, as a unit of consciousness, observe phenomena without being pulled hither and yon. The scientist seeks neither belief or faith but concrete, exact, precise knowledge.

"This is the ray of science and of research. The man on this ray will possess keen intellect, great accuracy in detail, and will make unwearied efforts to trace the smallest fact to its source, and to verify every theory. He will generally be extremely truthful, full of lucid explanation of facts, though sometimes pedantic and wearisome from his insistence on trivial and unnecessary verbal minutiae. He will be orderly, punctual, business-like, disliking to receive favors or flattery.

"It is the ray of the great chemist, the practical electrician, the first-rate engineer, the great operating surgeon. As a statesman, the fifth ray man would be narrow in his views, but he would be an excellent head of some special technical department, though a disagreeable person under whom to work. As a soldier, he would turn most readily to artillery and engineering. The artist on this ray is very rare, unless the fourth or seventh be the influencing secondary rays; even then, his coloring will be dull, his sculptures lifeless, and his music (if he composes) will be uninteresting, though technically correct in form. His style in writing or speaking will be clearness itself, but it will lack fire and point, and he will often be long-winded, from his desire to say all that can possibly be said on his subject." (*Esoteric Psychology*, v.i, pp. 208-9.)

**The Sixth Ray of Idealism and Devotion**. This energy gives rise to the "devotee type, full of idealism" (*Eso. Psych.*, v. 1, 329).

One finds the devotee in all walks of life—the religious devotee, the national-political devotee (the nationalist, the patriot), the ideological devotee (the loyalist), the person who is devoted to a charismatic leader, etc. There is generally a sensing of an ideal—a promise of things to come—followed by a dedication to that ideal.

In some respects, this is the ray about which we know the most, since collectively and cyclically it has been with us for a very long time. In other respects, it is difficult to recognize this ray energy as being part of ourselves, for we prefer to think that we proceed from intelligence and knowledge rather than a somewhat blind adherence to a sensed ideal.

Any new movement, whether religious, political, or scientific, etc., requires devotees, or those who sense the vision and who are willing to work in a self-sacrificing manner in order to manifest the visionary ideal. On a lesser scale, a person may simply be utterly devoted to the welfare of his/her family. Or a person may be an extraordinary devoted employee.

*The idea*, or archetypal form and divine pattern, *becomes the ideal* when clothed in the watery element of aspiration and desire. *We cognize the idea, and we feel the ideal.*

The sixth ray idealist moves towards the fourth ray of intuition and the second ray of love. The sixth ray type senses something that transcends intellect. Reason will often not move the idealist, since one feels that one is responding to something higher than reason. This explains why a person can lose a debate but not change his/her mind.

Devotion and idealism can transform the psychological condition rapidly, with immediate changes following in the physical condition. An example of this would be "falling on love." Another example would be a religious conversion:

14

Overnight wanton and selfish ways are relinquished and a new worker for the good suddenly emerges.

"This is called the ray of devotion. The man who is on this ray is full of religious instincts and impulses, and of intense personal feeling; nothing is taken equably. Everything, in his eyes, is either perfect or intolerable; his friends are angels, his enemies are very much the reverse; his view, in both cases, is formed not on the intrinsic merits of either class, but on the way the persons appeal to him, or on the sympathy or lack of sympathy which they show to his favorite idols, whether these be concrete or abstract, for he is full of devotion, it may be to a person, or it may be to a cause.

"He must always have a 'personal God,' an incarnation of Deity to adore. The best type of this ray makes the saint, the worst type, the bigot or fanatic, the typical martyr or the typical inquisitor. All religious wars or crusades have originated from sixth ray fanaticism. The man on this ray is often of gentle nature, but he can always flame into fury and fiery wrath. He will lay down his life for the objects of his devotion or reverence, but he will not lift a finger to help those outside of his immediate sympathies. As a soldier, he hates fighting but often when roused in battle fights like one possessed. He is never a great statesman nor a good business man, but he may be a great preacher or orator." (*Eso..Psych.* v. i, 209.)

**The Seventh Ray of Organization, Ceremonial Order or Magic.** This energy gives rise to the "business type full of organizing power and given to ritualistic ceremony" (*Eso. Psych*, v. i, p. 329). The seventh ray type may have less energy than the third ray type, but the seventh ray (unlike the third ray) will always having everything in order.

Ritual and ceremony can be understood in a variety of ways. Ritual includes our daily habits that enable us to get up in the morning, prepare breakfast (in an organized kitchen), and get to work on time. There are mating rituals, work rituals, dining rituals, recreational rituals, etc. *Ritual helps us to organize our physical plane life.*

Having a weekly meeting at a certain designated time is a ritual. Having a yearly conference is a ritual. Sowing seeds in the spring is a ritual. *Ritual helps us to function in a group way.*

One might say that ritual *looking downward* is organizing the physical plane life. Ritual *looking outward* is functioning in a group way. And ritual *looking upward* is sanctifying our participation in life.

The sanctifying of life can be done in the meaningful religious or spiritual ritual. This is perhaps the most important quality of this ray energy for it has to do with the *linking of spirit and matter.* The ceremonial form, as it replicates spiritual relationship, provides a focal point through which the higher energy can flow. This is experienced as a radiance bringing about psychic elevation. Right sound, color, form, and movement all play a critically important role in rhythm, organization, ritual, and ceremony.

*Right ritual is invocative.* A well organized office evokes psychological order, just as a disorganized office evokes the disorder of the frustration of wasted time. Nature's seasonal rituals evoke a psychological springing forth and a winter withdrawal. The ritual of the game evokes a team spirit. The communal voicing of the Lord's Prayer—*Thy will be done on earth as it is in heaven*—invokes Deity's blessing.

*The seventh ray is a ray of synthesis.* This suggests not only a unity, a wholeness, but also a fusing into one being. The distinction between one person in the group and another is lost as the group functions as a perfectly coordinated unit. The distinction between form and spirit is lost as the form becomes a perfect expression of spirit.

It is also interesting to realize that the fourth ray is a ray of creative art, but also the seventh ray is related to artistic expression. The third ray is a ray of business, but also the organization abilities of the seventh ray brings much skill in the business world. The fifth ray is a ray of science, but also the seventh ray brings scientific, inventive ability. The second ray of love brings a healing ability, as it is related to the heart center,

16

the thymus gland and the immune system. The seventh ray, as it conditions the etheric body and the whole being, is also a ray of healing. The sixth ray is attracted to religion; the seventh ray bring the great power of ritual to religion. The first ray of power must have its organized physical plane center. The seventh ray is more than versatile, *it is synthesizing.*

"This is the ceremonial ray, the ray which makes a man delight in 'all things done decently and in order,' and according to rule and precedent. It is the ray of the high priest and the court chamberlain, of the soldier who is a born genius in organization, of the ideal commissary general who will dress and feed the troops in the best possible way. It is the ray of the perfect nurse for the sick, careful in the smallest detail, though sometimes too much inclined to disregard the patients' idiosyncrasies and to try and grind them in the iron mill of routine.

"It is the ray of form, of the perfect sculptor, who sees and produces ideal beauty, of the designer of beautiful forms and patterns of any sort; but such a man would not be successful as a painter unless his influencing ray were the fourth. The combination of four with seven would make the very highest type of artist, form and color being both in excelsis. The literary work of the seventh ray man would be remarkable for its ultra-polished style, and such a writer would think far more of the manner than of the matter in his work, but would always be fluent both in writing and speech. The seventh ray man will often be sectarian. He will delight in fixed ceremonials and observances, in great processions and shows, in reviews of troops and warships, in genealogical trees, and in rules of precedence." (E.P., 210-11)

# LIST OF KEYWORDS
# AND A SELF-EVALUATION QUIZ

**List of Keywords and Phrases**.   As mentioned in the first chapter, a different ray can condition the five vehicles of consciousness-form: soul, personality, mind, emotional body, and physical body.   There can be, therefore, as many as five rays influencing a person in a direct way.   In many cases, however, a ray will appear twice in a person's psychological equipment, so that four (and sometimes even three) rays will be the conditioning energies. An example might be: soul 2nd ray, personality 3rd ray, mental body 5th ray, astral body 6th ray, and physical body 3rd ray—also written II, 3, 5-6-3.   Another example might be VI, 3, 2-6-7.   An example given in the book Discipleship in the New Age is: L.D.O. with the rays II, 4, 4-2-7.   In that case there are three conditioning rays: 2, 4, and 7.   Another example given in the same book is : C.D.P. with the rays II, 6, 5-6-6.   (A 6th ray physical body would be very uncommon.)

Also, during various stages of development, there are periods or cycles when one "body" or "vehicle"—such as the mental body or the personality—will appear with special prominence.   One or two rays will stand out above the others.

Below are lists of keywords and phrases (compiled from the previous chapter) for each of the seven rays.   They are listed here to aid the reader in the self-evaluation quiz immediately following.

## FIRST RAY OF WILL AND POWER.
the power type
administrative skills
the executive—managerial skills
ability to govern
responsibility
leadership qualities
understanding power related issues
skill in handling people
strength, persistence, endurance, steadfastness

sense of justice
destructive
benevolent dictator
diplomatic
rules and regulations
policy and procedure
law and order
significance
broad overview
willpower
fearless of consequences
impersonality
indifferent to comment
    NEGATIVELY
ruthlessness
hardness
tyrannical
despotic
excessive personal ambition
cruelty
personal power
disregard for feelings of others
insensitive

## SECOND RAY OF LOVE-WISDOM

the love type
wisdom
fusing power
wise counselor
patience, sympathy, understanding
compassion, empathy
inclusiveness
unity
team player
caution
teaching ability
love of study

healing ability
calmness, peacefulness
supportive
qualities of the heart
desire for pure knowledge
desire for absolute truth
    NEGATIVELY
lack of energy
liking to be liked
personal popularity
longing for security
fearfulness
over-attachment
overprotective
over-absorption in study
lack of will
dependence

## THIRD RAY OF INTELLIGENT ACTIVITY

active type
manipulating energy
active intellect
reasoning ability
business ability
energetic
adaptability
planning
strategist, tactician
using just the right word
pronouncing the truth
theorist
imitative ability, the actor
    NEGATIVELY
manipulative
intellectualism
over-adaptability, chameleon-like
scheming

hyperactive, busy-ness
deceptive words
criticism
impractical ideas

## FOURTH RAY OF HARMONY THROUGH CONFLICT
artistic type
sense of color
sensitivity to beauty
creative ability
imagination
intuitive
poetic faculty
sense of humor
mediator between higher and lower
refiner of form
creative life-style
rapid evolution
struggle, conflict
harmony, serenity
quick recovery from losses
    NEGATIVELY
mood swings
unnecessary conflicts
exaggeration
overly dramatic
inaccuracy
fluctuation between extreme moods
unrest
reskless
perpetual inner warfare
procrastination
easily overwhelmed by sorrow

## FIFTH RAY OF SCIENTIFIC KNOWLEDGE
scientific type
determines cause and effect relationship

technical ability
specialization
accuracy in detail
master a field of knowledge
precision
analytical
lucid explanation of fact
proving and verifying
detachment
ability to observe impartially
keen intellect
truthful
love of research
orderly
punctual
business-like
    NEGATIVELY
narrowness
over-specialization
intellectual pride
pedantic
may lack fire and point

## SIXTH RAY OF DEVOTION AND IDEALISM

devotee type
idealistic
high aspirations
mystic sense
visionary
dedicated
loyal
reverent
willing to live and die for a cause
religious instincts
love
self-effacing
self-sacrificing

humble
intense personal feeling
saintly
purity
gentle nature but can flame into fury
    NEGATIVELY
fanaticism
devotion to a personal god
bigotry
martyr complex
exclusive vision
frenzied follower
over leaning on others
seeing things as either perfect or intolerable
tunnel vision
blind adherence to an ideal
the inquisitor

## SEVENTH RAY OF ORGANIZATION
### AND CEREMONIAL ORDER

business type
order out of chaos
delight in ceremony
group work
practicality
empowering through ritual
synthesizing ability
skill in several areas
designer of beautiful forms
diplomatic
doing things decently and in order
working with rule and precedent
a sense of the magical
linking spirit with matter
understanding role of sound, color, and movement
delight in holiday ritual
understanding power of group invocation

23

beauty of form and pattern
NEGATIVELY
superstition
formalism
narrowness
sectarian
materialistic attitudes

**Self-Evaluation Quiz.** Some of the ray energies are present within us in varying degrees. Very tentatively we are going to assign a numerical value to the seven ray energies in a relative and approximate sense, as we try to gauge their influence or presence in our lives.

Review the ray lists above. Then give yourself a numerical value for each of the seven rays according to the following 0-to-10 scale.

0 - I do not detect the presence of this ray in my psychological equipment. In fact, sometimes I seem to have an antipathy for this ray energy.
1 - Negligible.
2 - Occasional traces.
3 - Some but not much.
4 - Presence felt somewhere.
5 - Presence with me some of the time.
6 - Qualities definitely in my psychological make-up.
7 - Developing attraction, presence often felt.
8 - A significant and determining influence in my life.
9 - Key factor, guiding influence, clear development.
10 - In abundance, very strong, major influence,
    my whole life, cannot live without it.

**Recording the Results**.

Ray One value:  [    ]

Ray Two value: [    ]

Ray Three value: [    ]

Ray Four value: [    ]

Ray  Five value:  [    ]

Ray Six Value:  [    ]

Ray Seven value: [    ]

add 5 to even no. [ 5 ]

ODD TOTAL_____          EVEN TOTAL_____

Add the numerical value for the odd numbered rays (odd total).
Add the numerical value for the even numbered rays and add an additional "5" (even total).

This very simple and cursory self-evaluation is at best merely suggestive of a predominance of ray energies along the 1-3-5-7 line or the 2-4-6 line, or it is an indication that there is a balance along these two major lines of ray energy.

Add the **grand total**, the total of all the rays, the even and the odd.  If your total is over 42, you are either highly developed or you are over-estimating your ray energies.

Find the **numerical difference between the odd and even totals**.  If that difference is *less than 10*, there is the likelihood of a *balance* of ray energy along the two major lines.  If the difference is *more than 15*, there is the likelihood that you are a *pronounced* ray type along one of the two major lines of ray energy.

The *balanced ray type* will be able to function well in a variety of settings.  The balanced type will probably get along well both at work and at home and will be able to function well with a variety of different types of people.  The balanced type will tend to be broad-minded, tolerant and inclusive, generally speaking.

The *pronounced ray types* can bring to their fields of interest the special asset of being highly developed and refined in certain areas.  They may, however, lack understanding of the other ray line of energies, and they may have difficulty realizing this deficiency.  Pronounced types would have to be more careful about the negative traits of their ray energies.

An *imbalanced person along the 1-3-5-7 line* would have to be very careful about becoming too hard, too cold, too detached, too insensitive, too ambitious in a personal and selfish way, too self-empowering, too materialistic. This type might have to work hard to include the softer values of love, compassion, sensitivity, and spiritual ideals.

An *imbalanced person along the 2-4-6 line* would have to very careful about becoming too fanatical, too other-worldly, too mystical, too visionary in an impractical and unrealistic way, too withdrawn, too dependent on others for their own material needs, and too sensitive to the short-comings of other people. This type would need to "toughen up" and work through the hardships of life without self-pity in order to gain greater strength, greater variety of skill, and greater self-reliance.

**The Two Major Lines of Ray Energy**. *Rays one, three, and seven* "are the great rays connected with form, with the evolutionary process, with the intelligent functioning of the system, and with the laws controlling the life in all forms in all the kingdoms in nature." It is also mentioned that rays one, three, and seven "deal with things concrete and with the functioning of matter and form from the lowest plane to the highest."

In contrast, *rays two, four, and six* are "connected with the inner life, expanding through the forms." They are the "rays of motive, aspiration, and sacrifice." They are rays "pre-eminently of quality." Rays two, four, and six "deal with things abstract, with spiritual expression through the medium of form." (*Esoteric Psychology*, v. i, p. 89.)

The fifth ray of science is sometimes considered along with the 1-3-5-7 line of ray energies, and sometimes it is considered as standing at a midpoint, forming "the connecting link of intelligence."

Listing the keywords from the above paragraph, we have:

| *Rays 1-3-7* | *Rays 2-4-6* |
|---|---|
| form | quality |
| evolutionary process | inner life |
| intelligent functioning | aspiration |
| functioning of the system | sacrifice |
| laws | motive |
| things concrete | things abstract |
| functioning of matter | spiritual expression |

Listing the types from the previous discussion, we have:

| *Rays 1-3-5-7* | *Rays 2-4-6* |
|---|---|
| the power type | the love type |
| the active type | the artistic type |
| the scientific type | the devotee type |
| the business type | |

In our study of the seven rays, there are certain re-occurring themes of which we should be mindful. The most fundamental is *to know thyself.* The effort here is to see ourselves as units of energy and as beings of quality—soul quality. Within the energy of one's ray qualities are *great archetypical themes, purposes, and meaning.* We become conscious of some of these themes as we consider the lives of *great souls.* Also, deep within ourselves we feel or sense the possibility of great accomplishments and deeply meaningful realizations. It is for us to come to know and to actualize the high being that we are.

Another re-occurring theme is that of *knowing the other.* This is the spouse, the brother, the neighbor, the work colleague, the person of different religion, different racial background, different gender, and different nationality. As the rays help us to understand ourselves, they also help us in a greater way to understand those who are not like us. Major psychological barriers between man and man can be torn asunder.

27

A third most important theme is that of *wholeness*. We are scrutinizing the part for purposes of becoming whole. We are developing a valuable quality in order to make a gift to the whole. Each developed quality brings us closer to health, harmony, and wholeness.

# A PRACTICAL EXAMPLE:
## DR. JARD DeVILLE'S
## PERSONALITY PATTERNS OF LEADERSHIP
## COMPARED TO THE SEVEN RAYS

The question of type comes up again and again. Sometimes it comes up in a field of health. Are there certain personality types that make one susceptible to certain illnesses? It often comes up in the field of psychology. Carl Jung discussed at some length a system of types that included the introvert, the extrovert, the thinking type, the feeling type, the sensation type, and a blending of the above types. In the field of esoteric religion Rudolf Steiner made a profound analysis of the Cain type—the more aggressive tiller of the ground, the hard working industrious ones who seek to accomplish things by their own efforts—and the Abel type, the more gentle and passive shepherd, the one who sought God's guidance in everything.

In the field of business, the question of managerial types, styles of leadership, comes up again and again. It is always interesting to look at a system of psychological types and compare it to that of the seven rays typology. Dr. Jard DeVille's system of managerial types is a result of careful observation over several years. We consider it as he presented it, and then we see what additional light can be shed on his system through knowledge of the seven rays.

In his book *The Psychology of Leadership* Dr. Jard DeVille discusses four primary personality patterns. He refers to these four types as the Controlling, the Entertaining, the Supporting, and the Comprehending patterns.

**The Controlling Pattern**. The Controlling personality pattern is characterized by self-reliance and self-control. DeVille calls the type the "Controllers" and the Command specialists." They tend to be "assertive and dominant" in relationships. They are not particularly concerned about the feelings of others. They tend to

29

be action-oriented, cool or controlled, and they tend to be precise in their use of time. One of their major qualities is their willingness to "take risks." Controllers like to cut through any confusion and go straight to the action (decision) in the effort to get the most important job done in the shortest amount of time. They do not like introspective discussions or "small talk." They like to "move out on schedule," which means taking action at times without thorough knowledge. They use "directive methods" in managing people. They like to issue orders or instructions. According to Jard DeVille, the Controllers feel all the emotions that other types feel, but they conceal them from others.

What ray type seems to stand out above the others in this brief characterization? The first ray type of power and will has special ability to rule and govern. This is the ray that appears most similar to DeVille's Controller and Command specialist. Similiar to the Controller, the first ray type likes to keep the emotions under control, to be self-reliant, and to take certain risks in his/her action oriented approach. Many first ray types tend to be assertive and dominant, but some use a quieter, subtler form of diplomacy.

**Comprehending Pattern.** In contrast to the Controller, the Comprehender is much less willing to take risks and much more intent on gathering more information before taking action. In contrast to Command specialist, DeVille calls this typy Information specialists. In contrast to telling others what to do, they tend to "ask others what they are doing." They use a "scientific cause-and-effect approach to problem analysis." As Information specialists, they tend to use organized and logical thought when coming to a decision. They like leadership positions where they are free to "poke and pry" about, until they have thorough knowledge of the people, the product, and the procedure to be able to make logical and factual choices. They are not comfortable with "great cognitive leaps" that to them would seem reckless and illogical.

Comprehenders are concerned with "lowering the risks created by unproven assumptions." Unlike the first ray Controllers, they tend to be very cautious and tend not to jump to conclusions. They are similar to the Controllers in that they like to keep their emotions calm and controlled. During times of stress and pressure, cool emotions help them to get all the pertinent facts, and cool emotions aid them in effectively dissecting the problem so that there is an accurate interpretation of exactly what is happening in the organization. The Comprehender likes to gather factual information, and then he likes to lay out the problematical situation in precise terms before looking for a cause. He wants to fully comprehend the nature of the problem. In spite of the urgency of the moment, he takes time to make a logical, thoughtful appraisal.

It seems clearly evident which ray type and qualitative energy DeVille is identifying here. It is, of course, the scientific or fifth ray type. In fact, he himself uses the term "scientific" and "cause-and-effect approach."

A list of key phrases contrasting the Controllers and Comprehenders might be helpful at this point.

| CONTROLLERS (FIRST RAY) | COMPREHENDERS (FIFTH RAY) |
|---|---|
| telling others | asking others |
| issuing instructions | gathering information |
| risk taking | lowering risk with knowledge |
| action oriented | delaying action in order to gain more information |
| precise use of time | time to dissect problems |
| commanding | poking, prying |
| assertive, dominant | cause-and-effect approach |
| emotional control | emotional control |
| logical thought but sometimes jumps to conclusions | logical, organized thought |
| uncomfortable with introspection | uncomfortable with cognitive leaps |

**Entertaining Pattern.** Another type to which DeVille calls our attention deals with the Entertaining personality pattern. He refers to these people as Entertainers and Enthusiasts. These people have the tendency to be outspoken and to express themselves freely. They favor relationships and activities that are warm and close but on their own terms. They are not precise in their use of time. They are always willing to pause in their work and talk to people in an enthusiastic way. This is something that the people at the top tend not to understand.. This type is usually willing to accept some risk in terms of personal relationships, for they tend to be open and tend to reveal their feelings freely to other people.

The Controllers *tell others what to do.*

The Comprehenders *ask people what they are doing.*

The Enthusiasts *tell other what they are feeling.*

The Enthusiasts use emotion to inspire others to do their best for the sake of the work or the organization. They like to tell stories, share anecdotes, give parties, meet people, and speculate over possibilities. An extreme Entertainer type may cause confusion to the Comprehender and Controller. The Controllers and Comprehenders are more task oriented, the Enthusiastic is more people oriented.

In his analysis of managerial types, DeVille points out that all of these types have something valuable to contribute, and they can all learn something from each other. The Enthusiasts go beyond logic and objective systems. They try to create a climate of excitement and goodwill that inspires others to do their best. The Enthusiastic managers are like coaches who inspire a great team effort. They are quick to give praise but also quick to point out what needs to be corrected. They capture the imagination with their dreams of success. As they communicate their enthusiasm, they tend to offer "emotional rewards and draw people close to them in a community of achievers" (DeVille 102)

What type is Deville identifying here? Several qualities seem to point primarily to a fourth ray influence. The fourth ray influence could be a fourth ray personality, or even a strong fourth ray mind. (A fourth ray soul would be a remoter possibility.)

The word "entertaining" suggests a combination of artistic, dramatic, and emotional qualities. Both the fisrt ray Controllers and the fifth ray Comprehenders tend to emphasize emotional control and tend to be object or task oriented, rather than people oriented. This is in keeping to a degree with the relationship between the rays and the planes. The first and fifth ray types would tend to emphasize the mental plane (fifth ray) and the physical plane (seventh ray). This brings into play such qualities as mental clarity, logical thought, planning, organization, and a hierarchical chain-of-command. There may also be either a rejection or neglect of the emotional plane factors to some degree. The fourth ray type, on the other hand, has a greater affinity with the emotional plane, which is conditioned by the sixth ray of idealism. These two rays readily connect or relate along the 2-4-6 line of ray energies. The Entertainers will tend to bring in the emotional connection between people. They want to:

- draw people close
- feel close and warm
- feel the togetherness of the team spirit
- give enthusiastic praise
- be personable with people

Unlike the mental-physical alignment of the Controllers and Comprehenders who like to be impersonal, the Entertainers tend to want to more of a personal relationship.

With the fourth Ray of Harmony through Conflict, such qualities as team effort, closeness and warmth, entertainment through the use of humor, all relate to the *harmony* factor.

DeVille also mentions that the Entertainers tend to express themselves freely, tend to be outspoken, and tend to be quick in correcting others. These characteristics lean towards the *conflict* factor.

The fourth ray Entertainers, with all their desire for warmth and harmony, can be surprisingly undiplomatic at times. To understand them, however, one must realize that the fourth ray compels them towards an interplay of the polar opposites that eventually leads to harmony and unification. Conflict is a means of bringing the pain of underlying separation openly into consciousness, so that a harmony and a brotherhood may truly be sought. The great human tendency is to seek complacency and ease. The tendency of inertia is to remain in the lull of semiconsciousness. The shock of conflict stirs one out of the lull of habitual patterns.

Entertainers, according to DeVille, use the technique of telling stories and anecdotes. This is in contrast to the Controllers (first ray) and the Comprehenders (fifth ray) who both tend to stay more to the facts or concern themselves with the concrete task at hand. Stories can entertain; they can provide humor and a release of tension. Stories can provide insight as they point out the ironies of life. Story telling includes the emotional component to a large degree. The Entertainers or Enthusiastics captivate the imagination, inspire others, speculate over possibilities, and "create a climate of excitement." This is a far different energy than the power-control of the first ray type and far different than the knowledge-information of the fifth ray type.

From a first of fifth ray point of view, the fourth ray Entertainers may appear to be insufficiently task-oriented at times. The Enthusiastics generate an astral excitement as they reach for a nebulous something which is neither physical nor logical. It is important to recall that Enthusiastics are more people oriented than task oriented. Mentally, the Enthusiastics tend to think more speculatively and imaginatively than do the other two types. In some respects this may appear to be impractical, unrealistic, or illogical. On the other hand, the more imaginative approach can serve to loosen the rigidity of an over fixed or static system. New ideas, innovation direction, and fresh ways of viewing the work of the organization can come from the creative Entertainer (4th ray) type.

Below is a brief list emphasizing the differences between the Enthusiastics and Controllers.

| ENTHUSIASTICS (4TH RAY) | CONTROLLERS (5TH RAY) |
|---|---|
| outspoken | diplomatic |
| imaginative | unimaginative |
| inspiring | directing |
| imprecise use of time | precise use of time |
| people oriented | task oriented |
| enthusiastic team effort | chain of command |
| enjoy interacting | aloof interaction |
| personal | impersonal |
| reveal feelings | conceal feelings |

**Supporting Pattern.** The Supporters are "loyal," "agreement oriented and consensus seeking." They are often generous with their time, willing to help others understand a problem, situation, or solution. The Supporters tend to relate to others with "friendship and love." They prefer not to take any risks that would hurt a relationship. In their effort to avoid the pain of criticizing a friend or colleague, they tend to tolerate situations even when there is a great need to correct them. This type, according to DeVille, tends to "work through people in an indirect, accepting manner," rather than focusing directly on the tasks.

The Supporters or Loyals are similar to the Enthusiastics in that they ask others what they are feeling. They are more people oriented than task oriented. They are, however, less aggressive than the Enthusiastics. The latter tend to force themselves on others at times. Supporters are accepting, encouraging, and tend to be "low-key."

The Supporters and the 1st ray Controllers may have the same goals of higher productivity and increased quality, but their way of achieving it is quite different. Being people oriented, the Supporters see increased quality as the logical outcome of cooperation and a mutually supportive attitude. One does not have to place the end task as the primary objective. Treat people well and they will naturally perform better. Treat them like machines and the subsequent resentment will interfere with quality work.

To the Controllers, this may seem a poor way of dealing with people. The Controllers focus on the objective and tend to disregard the "atmospherics" of good feelings. Feelings are to be controlled or overcome or disregarded, much as an athlete might disregard them in the discipline of the training routine. The Controllers "force people to adapt willy-nilly without regard to feelings and needs" (DeVille, 123, 124).

The strong points of the Loyal or Supporting type manager include the ability to guide or teach other workers and managers. The Supporting manager is similar to the counselor or psychologist. They help people grow and mature in the job.

What ray would one assign to the Supporter or Loyal type? Even though the word "loyal" draws attention to the 6th ray of idealism and devotion, it is the 2nd ray of love-wisdom that seems to be the predominant energy identified here by DeVille.

There are certain similarities between the Supporters (2nd ray) and the Enthusiastics (4th ray). Unlike the Controllers and Comprehenders, who prefer to ignore or eliminate the emotional factor in dealing with the task at hand, both the Enthusiatics and the Supporters include the emotional factor in their people oriented approach. Both try to generate a warm and accepting atmosphere of support and friendship. They take time to deal with people problems as well as task problems.

The Supporters differ from the Enthusiastics, in that the former tend to be low-key, whereas the Entertainers tend to be outspoken, witty, and good story tellers. Also the entertainment quality may have a 4th ray pendulum swing to it. Sometimes the joke is carried too far. Sometimes gloomy silences occur between the scintillating brilliance. The Supporters would tend to be consistently non-confrontative, whereas the Entertainers would tend to fluctuate between conflict and harmony.

THE SUPPORTERS (2ND RAY)
    agreement oriented
    consensus seeking
    willing to help

36

generous with time
cooperative
team players
counseling people
recognizing others skills
avoiding risks that might hurt others
encouraging others
emotional support
good listeners
concern with feelings
non-aggressive
low-key
an accepting manner
friendship and love
people oriented

**The Benefits of DeVille's System.** One of the major points DeVille is trying to make is that the old authoritarian form of leadership is inadequate in contemporary society. The hard-line Controlling pattern is antiquated. DeVille uses Henry Ford II as an example of a dominant Controller type. An extreme type will tend to attract and promote similar types around him. In DeVille's judgment, the Ford Company under Henry Ford II almost ended in disaster because "the management team was not introspective enough to discover what was going on in the emotions of the people who buy automobiles."

DeVille was trying to point out that each type can learn from each other. Each type should try to develop as many of the qualities of other types as possible. Remaining in one's own "comfort zone" can have a crippling effect on the work team.

Since traditionally businesses have functioned primarily under the Controlling pattern, DeVille advocates the use of methods and techniques that come more naturally to the Supporting and Enthusiastic personality pattern. The psychological or people oriented approach is a necessary complement to the task oriented approach.

**Inadequacies of DeVille's System.** DeVille's recommendations to businessmen seem very well researched and very sound. His psychological system of types, however, seems to have certain limitations when viewed in the light of the seven rays.

DeVille's system deals with four basic types; in esoteric psychology we are told that there are seven. In DeVille's system one seems to be basically one type or another, with the option of acquiring some of the characteristics of the other types. In esoteric psychology one can more readily see how one can embody the qualitative energy of two, three, or even four types (relatively speaking). As mentioned earlier, a different ray can condition the soul, the personality, and the three aspects of personality (mental, emotional, and physical bodies). One can have the predominant and blended energies of two rays, with traces of a third or fourth type.

In examining types from a scientific perspective it is desirable to have something approaching a "pure type." Examining this matter strictly from the outer world of appearances, from observable characteristics, as DeVille seems to do, has its disadvantages in that outwardly there is no "pure type." At best we look for what might be called "pronounced types" in order to see a relatively clear example of a particular type. Is there anything else we can do besides try to identify and sort out the complex overlapping of various outward characteristics and behaviors? Another possibility would be to consider the archetypal patterns as given on the seven rays in esoteric psychology, at least in a hypothetical way. The pure type, accessible to our meditative and archetypal perception, helps us understand and sort out the obscurations of blended energies, as they appear in the three worlds (physical-emotional-mental) of human endeavor.

It is interesting to note that in DeVille's four types—Controller, Comprehender, Enthusiasitc, and Supporter—we find the three rays that generally condition the mind or mental vehicle:

1st ray mind, administrative type...... Controller
4th ray mind, creative, artistic.......... Enthusiastic
5th ray mind, scientific type............ Comprehender

It is also interesting to note that in DeVille's four-type system there is a nice balance along the two lines of ray energy:

*Tougher Line—Task Oriented, 1-3-5-7*
    Controller.............. 1st Ray
    Comprehender....... 5th Ray

*Softer Line—People Oriented, 2-4-6*
    Enthusiastic........... 4th Ray
    Supporter.............. 2nd Ray

What is basically suggested here is that DeVille himself is probably a people-oriented type. He sees the inclusion of the important people-sensitive management styles as replacing some of the out-dated hard-line approaches.

DeVille advises managers to develop a "true partnership with employees. Form a mutually supportive relationship that harnesses the psychological and spiritual needs, which are so often ignored by companies because they [the needs] are subjective rather than objective." (DeVille, 184.)

# The Three Rays of Aspect
## and the Four Rays of Attribute

Rays 1-2-3 (Will-Love-Intelligence) are the *three rays of aspect*. This is comparable to the Trinity.

Rays 4-5-6-7 (Harmony-Science-Idealism-Organization) are the *four rays of attribute*.

Along with the two lines of ray energy—the even line (2-4-6) and the odd numbered line (1-3-5-7)—the Aspect-Attribute "division" helps considerably in understanding some of the dynamics of the seven ray energies.

The three *rays of aspect* are "the expression of the creative purpose, and the synthesis of life, quality and appearance.... Through them the differentiated forms come into being." (*Esoteric Psychology*, v. 1, 158.)

The four rays of attribute "find their synthesis in the third ray of aspect." (See diagram below.) The four rays of attribute produce "the varying qualities in greater detail than do the three rays of aspect." (EP, v.1, 162.)

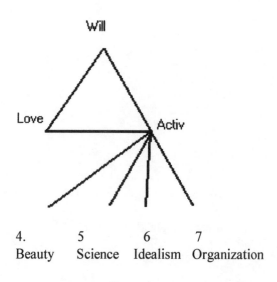

40

THREE RAYS OF ASPECT:
- creative purpose
- synthesis of life-quality-appearance

FOUR RAYS OF ATTRIBUTE:
- greater detail of qualities
- find synthesis in third ray

It might be easier to grasp this important distinction if we were to consider ways of drawing out the above qualities in an educational setting. The creative *arts*, the aesthetic sense (4th ray) and the *idealistic-devotional* attitude (6th ray) would probably be much easier to cultivate than would *love-wisdom* (2nd ray).

Similarly, the more detailed *scientific mode* of operation (5th ray) might be more accessible to educational method than the more general *intelligence* of the 3rd ray. Also, 7th ray *organization* is far more specific that the more elusive 1st ray of *power*.

In some respects, then, it should be considerably easier to "see" or to recognize the manifested play of the four rays of attribute than the three rays of aspect.

**A Case in Which the Rays of Aspect Predominate.** What would be the psychological implications of a case in which a person had predominantly the rays of aspect (1-2-3)? We found such a case in the book *Discipleship in the New Age*. The student W.D.S. had the following, rather unusual, ray equipment:

Soul............................ 2nd ray of Love-Wisdom
Personality................... 1st ray of Will or Power.
   mind........................... 2nd ray, Love-Wisdom.
   astral body................... 1st ray, Will or Power.
   physical body................ 3 rd ray, Active Intelligence.

This is a very unusual situation. The 2nd ray mind is an exception to the general rule of 1, 4 or 5. The 1st ray astral is an exception to the general rule of ray 2 or 6. Of the 41 students discussed in the book, W.D.S. is the only one who has all of his bodies or vehicles on the first three rays of aspect.

D.K.'s following words of advice help us understand something of the dynamics involved:

> You would profit much if you studied carefully the rays which are, at this time, lacking in your equipment. The forces of the 4th, 5th, 6th, 7th rays are not present. All your rays are major rays of aspect. The rays of attribute are lacking and hence your problem and your immense opportunity. What saves the situation for you is that in a previous life, you worked through a fourth ray personality. Harmony through Conflict is, with you, a deep-seated desire and a basic determination. You have inherited it and in it your present life is rooted.
>
> One of the best ways in which you can learn to solve your problem is to train yourself to be—as are all true hierarchical workers—the one in the background, and not the one at the centre. You will still be the one, for you are still a personality, but you can learn to work silently and through love, and carry all forward from the background. You will then gradually become a hidden force, galvanizing others into activity and pushing them forward in their work, offering them their needed opportunity and training, but in complete self-forgetfulness. (*Discipleship in the New Age*, v. 1, 379, 380)

There are several very important esoteric psychological factors mentioned in the above two paragraphs.

1) A person can draw upon and utilize the ray qualities developed in a previous incarnation, even when his/her present bodies are not conditioned by that ray. This implies, however, that a ray quality from a pervious life reached a relatively high degree of development and refinement.

2) Having all one's bodies on the rays of aspect is both a "problem" and an "immense opportunity." The problem would probably have to do with the difficulty of manifesting one's energy through points of contact in the three worlds of human endeavor.

Wisdom or Power without a means of expression or without points of outlet would lead to unmanifested, congested, or blocked energy. This could lead to psychological and physiological disorders.

The "immense opportunity" might have to do with what could be called the power and understanding of wholeness. To understand the whole (to have a holistic sense) one must have a feel for and knowledge of triplicities. The relative whole unit works through triplicitiies. Power alone is extremely dangerous and can lead to self-destruction. Wisdom alone can be ineffectual. Intelligence alone is often much activity signifying nothing. But power used wisely with loving understanding, and power that has an intelligent base and an intelligent operation is, to use the above phrase, an *immense opportunity.*

Even when one has the first two rays—will-Purpose and Love-Wisdom—along with one of the rays of attribute, we see something of the same *immense opportunity* mentioned in respect to the three major rays. It is the opportunity to be closer to the larger picture, the Grand Design, the Plan of Deity.

The *three rays of aspect,* symbolized by the triangle in the circle, when present in a psychological unit, or when truly present in a *group endeavor,* greatly facilitate a labor of profound significance and meaning.

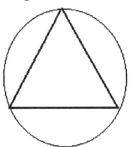

In this regard it is most interesting that the rays given for the Buddha and the Christ are one, two, and six. The sixth ray of idealism and devotion was the major ray conditioning the entire Piscean Age. In the Aquarian Age it stands to reason that rays one, two, and seven would carry extraordinary significance. (See *The Destiny of Nations,* 138-9.)

The power and significance of the triplicities—as they approximate the three rays of aspect—should not be underestimated.

**The Seven Planes**. Considering this matter of the rays of aspect and attribute from the point of view of the *seven planes*, again the rays of attribute are more "visible" or easier to discern:

> The rays of attribute exist "in degrees on all the planes, but they have their particular emphasis in the evolution of the reincarnating ego in the three worlds at this time. These four Rays control, in a subtle and peculiar manner, the four kingdoms of nature—mineral, vegetable, animal and human—and at their merging into the three Rays of Aspect . . . have a correspondence with the merging of man (the product of the three kingdoms and the fourth) into the superhuman kingdom, the spiritual. *Treatise on Cosmic Fire* 588.

The three rays of aspect condition the highest or subtlest planes—the plane of Adi, the Monadic plane, and the Atmic plane. These three refined and elevated planes are far beyond the present reach of the vast majority. They do, however, have their correspondence on all of the seven planes.

Each of the seven planes have a seven sub-plane strata. (See diagrams on the following pages.) *The three highest sub-planes of each of the seven planes do have a correspondence with the first three rays of aspect.*

On the physical plane, the highest three sub-planes would be the first three etheric sub-planes. (See diagram.)

On the mental plane, *the soul "resides" on the higher sub-planes of the mental plane.* (See diagram of egoic lotus.)

| | |
|---|---|
| ADI | 1st |
| Monadic Plane  Spirit or Monad | 2nd |
| Atmic Plane  Spiritual Will | 3rd |
| Buddhic Plane  Plane of Intuition | 4th |
| Mental Plane  Higher Mind  Soul | 5th |
| Lower Mind, Intellect | |
| Astral Plane  Plane of Emotion | 6th |
| Three aspects of Personality | |
| Etheric Plane  with its 4 etheric sub-planes | 7th |
| gaseous sub-plane  liquid sub-plane  dense physical sub-plane | |

The SEVEN PLANES  each with 7 sub-planes

The Mental Plane is a dual plane. The higher sub-planes are known as the abstract mental plane (arupa). The lower sub-planes are known as the concrete mental plane (rupa)—the plane of intellect.

The Physical Plane is also a dual plane. The four higher sub-planes are known as the etheric sub-planes. Magnetism and electricity are probably related to the 4th ether. The densest three planes are the gaseous, liquid, and dense physical sub-planes.

Only the latter two sub-planes are visible to normal human sight. Clairvoyant sight can see forms, colors, energy strands and a host of beings on of the higher planes.

For a color representation of the higher planes as seen by a clairvoyant, the reader is referred to the book *Man Visible and Invisible* by Charles W. Leadbeater.

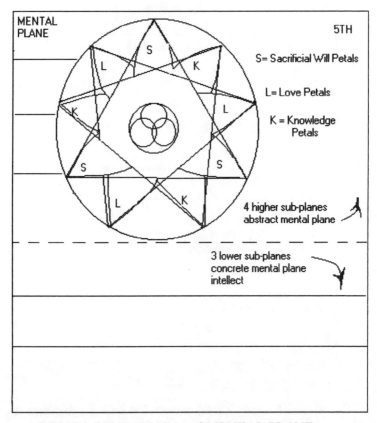

MENTAL PLANE

5TH

S= Sacrificial Will Petals

L= Love Petals

K = Knowledge Petals

4 higher sub-planes abstract mental plane

3 lower sub-planes concrete mental plane intellect

EGOIC LOTUS (SOUL) and MENTAL PLANE
( See *Treatise on Cosmic Fire* for more detailed diagrams.)

**The Soul (Egoic Lotus)** is on the abstract levels of the mental plane. "The definition of the soul may be regarded as somewhat more feasible than that of spirit owing to the fact that there are many people who have experienced at sometime or another an illumination, an unfoldment, an uplifting, and a beatitude which has convinced them that there is a state of consciousness so far removed from that normally experienced as to bring them into a new state of being and a new level of awareness. It is something felt and experienced, and involves that psychic expansion which the mystic has registered down the ages . . . .

1. The soul, macrocosmic and microcosmic, universal and human, is that entity which is brought into being when the spirit aspect and the matter aspect are related to each other.

a. The soul therefore is neither spirit nor matter but is the relation between them.

b. The soul is the mediator between this duality; it is the middle principle, the link between God and His form.

c. Therefore the soul is another name for.the Christ principle, whether in nature or in man." *Treatise on White Magic* 34-35.

The soul has been symbolically compared to a lotus flower. There are three layers of petals, with three petals in each layer. Again we have very important *sets of triplicities.*

Generally speaking, the *knowledge petals* of the soul unfold first. This has to do with the important factor of *light.* Metaphorically (or perhaps not metaphorically), one is moving from *darkness into light.*

In some cases the *love petals* of the soul are unfolded first. There is a fluid dynamic in the gradual process of soul unfoldment and consciousness expansion. There is a rhythm and there are patterns, but there is also great fluidity. The unfoldment of the love stage has to do with the movement from the *unreal to the real.*

The third set of petals of the egoic lotus to open are the sacrificial petals. "The 'petals of sacrifice' unfold and the sacred sacrificial aspect of life is revealed in its beauty, purity, simplicity and in its revolutionizing quality." *Cosmic Fire* 31.

We should take special notice of *purity* and *simplicity* as being key qualities of the will aspect.

The Personality also has a threefold nature:

MENTAL BODY or INTELLECT
ASTRAL BODY or Sentient Body
PHYSICAL-ETHERIC BODY

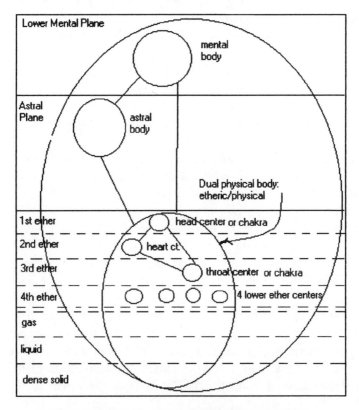

THE THREE PLANES OF PERSONALITY

As well as the mind-astral-physical triplicity, there is the very important triplicity on the etheric plane of the three higher chakras or etheric centers—Head Chakra...Heart Chakra....Throat Chakra.

Here we have, generally speaking, the three rays of aspect, or a potential access to the three rays of aspect, within the energy body of a human being.

48

**Summary**.  The seven ray subject matter is concerned with Quality, Consciousness, Unity, and Wholeness.  In order to understand Wholeness, it is necessary to see how the Whole naturally divides or separates into the archetypal triplicities.  This separation is apparent in form manifestation, but from a more elevated awareness, there is no separation.

The head chakra, the heart chakra, and the throat chakra—as they relate to the pineal gland, thymus, and thyroid gland—perform separate and distinct functions, yet are vital parts of the whole body.

The Personality has its three major aspects: intellect, sentience or feeling, and physical body.  These three have a correspondence with the Sacrificial Will, Love, and Light of the Soul.

The three major rays (will-love-light) provide an immense opportunity when they are present in a developed way in any given individual.  This is a rare occurrence.  *When the first ray and second ray are present, one can think of the third aspect as being anyone of the rays of attribute.*  For example, 1-2-4, 1-2-5, 1-2-6, or 1-2-7 are all very powerful ray combinations.  One of the reasons for this is the ability to work in a whole way.

...................................................................................

In the following chapter we attempt to take a very practical look at the three Rays of Aspect as they stand behind the Threefold Social Order that is prevalent in human activity.

# The THREE RAYS OF ASPECT and the
# THREEFOLD SOCIAL ORDER

*We shall be working in a basically realistic way if all proper institutions begin aiming towards threefolding.*
Rudolf Steiner, *Conferences with Teachers.*

*Whether the forces of decline that exist in human evolution can be transformed into forces of ascent will depend on the introduction of the threefolding impulse into all the observable and transformable aspects of life.*
Rudolf Steiner, *The Cycle of the Year.*

**The Threefold Social Order.** Throughout all our books is the attempt to show the intense practicality of the esoteric teaching. Recognizing in some degree the *play of triplicities* within the relative whole—recognizing the threefolding process, or the "threefolding impulse"—is of great importance and practicality.

It stands to reason that if the seven rays condition and play though all aspects of manifested life, then these ray energies should be recognizable to some degree in the very forms that they condition and bring about.

In this chapter we consider the "Threefold Social Order" with the help of Rudolf Steiner's ideas on this fascinating subject.

The natural threefolding process gives rise to distinct "domains" in the social order. Steiner calls these three domains:

1. Government, or the Rights State (*Rechtsstaat*).
2. The Spiritual-Cultural Life.
3. The Economic Sphere.

*Government* has to do primarily with the question of *rights*. When people live in a group or community, out of necessity there has to be some kind of order. Order is partially established through a system of laws, statutes, rules, and regulations. Government, then, has to do with orderly community living.

50

The *spiritual-cultural domain* is an entirely different sphere of human life. This domain includes the religious life, the educational work, and the spiritual quest. It includes also art and science.

The *economic sphere* deals with the work of meeting humanities needs and wants. This sphere has to do with the production and distribution of goods and the organized delivery of services.

**The Keynotes of the Threefold Social Order** are *égalité, liberté, and fraternité*:

1. Government.......*Equality*. People are *equal* before the law. The law protects the rights of the individual living in the community.

2. Spiritual-Cultural Domain.....*Liberty or Freedom*. This has to do with the inner and individual relationship between a human being and God, between a human being and his or her soul. It has to do with the freedom of religion. It has to do with the freedom to express political ideas. Our worshiping of Deity is an inner and individual matter. It cannot be brought about through legislation. It cannot be bought and sold in the market place. It is essentially a sacred relationship.

3. The Economic Domain.......*Fraternity or Brotherhood*. The idea of brotherhood is a very important and very subtle factor. Brotherhood is a uniting of differences more than a merging of similarities. Out of necessity (not out of choice) we must work side-by-side with people of varied natures. After working side-by-side with other people over a period of time, we discover a certain *unity of differences*. In spite of the differences, we eventually awaken to the fact that we are all part of the same family of humanity.

**Money in the Threefold Social Order**. Money is a medium of exchange, a measure of value, and a means of payment. Basically, money is acquired and utilized in different ways in the three domains.

1. Government acquires money through *taxes*.
2. The Spiritual-Cultural Domain acquires money essentially through *contribution*.
3. The Economic Domain acquires money through the *production of goods*.

Money has been defined esoterically as "concretized energy." In the *Economic Domain* this "energy" is *generated through activity*. Through the use of the hands and the limbs, or the activity of the brain, things are fashioned that are of use to other people. This generates capital.

In the *Spiritual-Cultural Domain* the acquiring of money is more akin to *inspiration*. Here the effort is to present the vision, or to touch the heart, or to attend to the spiritual-cultural-educational edification of the people. The people then respond by giving, by contributing. There has been a tradition of something like a "vow-of-poverty" taken by people working in this realm. People working in this realm do generally make less money than those working in the other two realms. Personal sacrifices are made in order to live a life of service. The work in the other two domains, however, also constitutes great areas of potential service. Each of the three realms are equally important and vital to the well-being of the whole.

In the realm of *Government* money is *acquire through taxes*, which is related to the factor of power and law. Some say that government should be run like a business. Government, however, does not produce products, does not manufacture goods, and does not generate capital. An armed force is not a factory of workers. Their task is to stand prepared, ready to defend a nation. To stand in such a way is a factor of *power*, not a factor of business. In centuries past, an army often supported itself through pillage and plunder—a barbaric form of power. No national army could be supported in such a fashion in this day and age.

We have then the following correspondences:

*Money in the Three Domains:*

1. State............Taxes...............Power/Ruler...............the Head
2. Culture.........Contribution.....Inspiration.................the Heart
3. Economy......Production........Activity......................the Throat

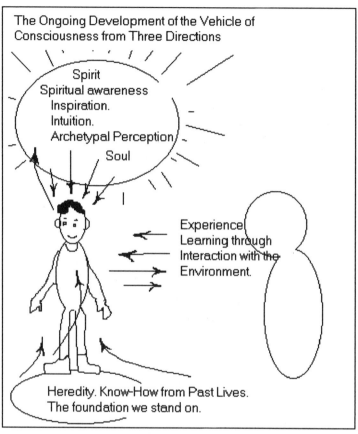

The Ongoing Development of the Vehicle of Consciousness from Three Directions

Spirit
Spiritual awareness
Inspiration.
Intuition.
Archetypal Perception.
Soul

Experience
Learning through
Interaction with the
Environment.

Heredity. Know-How from Past Lives.
The foundation we stand on.

We learn and are sustained from *below upward,* from *outward to inward,* and from *above downward.* The directional terms used here are three dimensional, and as such they are primarily metaphoric. The three "directions" are in actual fact multidimensional.

In our esoteric studies we are concerned with all of these "directions." In our discussion of the threefold social order, however, it is necessary to draw special attention to the direction along which inspiration comes. What we are concerned with here is *archetypal perception* or *spiritual insight.* Spiritual insight inspires humankind to explore certain new directions in all fields of endeavor.

53

Looking at the threefold social order from a certain angle, we could say that from *below upward* we are sustained by what has been commonly called *necessities of life*. This has to do with the physical necessities of food, shelter, clothing, etc. Upon these basic needs are added many additional wants that can be seen as a refined physical plane living.

From outward to inward, or from the *interaction* with the environment, we are *regulated by custom, by common law, and by rule of law*. There is something like a legal, contractual relationship—either explicit or implicit—that every communal person is require to live by. There is no such thing as a society of people without the governing of some kind of law. The law that governs some form of community living is a different kind of necessity of life than that provided by the economic domain.

From *above downward* we are sustained by the *vision* that indicates direction. *One cannot be sustained by bread alone. Without a vision the people perish.* This too then is a necessity of life, but of a different order. We have here the communication with our spiritual roots. Here we discern the meaning of life.

The tendency towards Threefoldness is evident in many social systems.

## THE TRIBAL SYSTEM

1. The Chief. The Elders. The leader with his/her advisers.
   The "army" of braves and warriors.
2. The Shaman. The healers, the "medicine men."
   Those responsible for the ceremony, the vision.
3. The food produces, the farmers, the hunters, the craft workers.

## THE MEDIEVAL SYSTEM

1. The King or Duke and his court.
   The knights or warriors under the direction of the king.
2. The Church. The Church hierarchy, cardinals, bishops, priests. The monks and nuns responsible for education, copying manuscripts, teaching, maintaining libraries.
3. The Merchants. The Artisans and Laborers.

This tripartite, functional division during the Middle Ages was also known as the *bellatores*, the *oratores*, and the *laboratores*—or those who *fight*, those who *pray*, and those who *labor*.

The *bellatores* were the warriors, the horsemen. They gathered around a leader or *dominus*. In order to enter into their circle one had to demonstrate strength and the ability to withstand pain. The new nobility emerged out of the elite within this group. A chivalric knighthood developed whose duty it was to protect the other two orders with their arms.

The *oratores* were the clergy and the monks. Their main responsibility was prayer. This connected them with the spiritual world and gave them a special authority on earth. They were the interpreters of the divine will and purpose. They were in the early Middle Ages the only ones who were educated. The noblemen of the warrior class were, initially, not able to read and write. The monks had to learn how to read. They were required to spend two to three hours daily doing spiritual reading. The church or the monastery was the center of culture.

The *laboratores* were the peasant class, the producers. They tilled the soil, sowed the seed, harvested the crop. They raised sheep, goats, pigs, and fowl. They produced cheese, wine, beer, and cider. They pruned fruit orchards, developed vineyards, olive groves, and nut trees. They used horses, ox, and mules in their work. They milled grain. Some became blacksmiths. They used a large number of iron implements.

The artisans and the merchants developed and grew in number and sophistication. Guilds were organized, each with its own set of special skills and abilities. In the Middle Ages the artisans were put primarily at the service of the Church. Paintings were seen as a religious lesson for people who could not read. The artist was considered a manual laborer. Works of art were not signed. There were architects, stone masons, sculptors, goldsmiths, glass workers, metal casters, parchment makers, calligraphers, and painters.

During the beginning of the Middle Ages, we find primarily an agrarian society—most people were peasants and most worked the land. The merchant was a secondary element in the economic domain. The merchant class gradually grew in importance and eventually was a key factor in changing the whole feudal system.

*The rays help one to understand the natural divisions of the social order, since the divisions are essentially along qualitative lines. At the same time, however, it is important to realize that all the rays can be found within each social domain.*

**The Separation of Powers, the Right Relationship Between the Three Domains.** The Church had a great deal of power during the Middle Ages. From an esoteric point of view, it must be remembered that *the Sixth Ray of Idealism and Devotion was the major ray during the Piscean Age.* (During the emerging Aquarian Age, it is the Seventh Ray of Organization and Ceremonial Magic that holds the position of major ray for the approximately 2000 year Age.) With the Sixth Ray as being the major influence during the Piscean Age, it is understandable that religion, in one form or another, played a dominant role—and also an *interfering* role.

But here we come to a most important point that needs to be appreciated. It has to do with the *separation of powers*, or putting it a better way, it has to do with the *non-interference of one domain to another*. Or to express it in a still better way: It has to do with the *right relationship between domains*.

If we look at the natural tendency towards a threefold social order during the Middle Ages, we see that for a considerable period of time the Church had more power and influence than the predominantly agrarian Economic Domain. We see the Church also as controlling many factors of State. To cite briefly one example: In 1302 Pope Boniface VIII issued a bull, *Unam Sanctam*, reaffirming in the strongest terms the *supremacy of the pope over secular rulers*. King Philip IV of France, however, was strong enough to defy the power of the Church. He responded to the papal bull by sending a small army to Italy to capture the pope and force his resignation. At this political point (as well as several others) the separation of Church and State started to move forward. The Church's interference in matters of state was a leitmotiv of the Middle Ages. One could say that this interference was everywhere and almost all the time.

Why do we need separation (or non-interference)? For the same reason the heart is not a kidney and the lungs are not the brain. The different units perform different functions, albeit they are part of the same body.

**A Healthy or Sick Society.** The word "health" has special significance here. Steiner emphasized that we should not look at social issues as being "good" or "evil", rather we should look at them as being "healthy" or "unhealthy." That should help to avoid some of the complications and zealousness of political party affiliation. Both parties need carefully to consider what in truth constitutes a truly healthy society. We have to be able to look at the many "sick" or unhealthy factors in the society, and then we have to be able to work together and have the political will to do something about them.

In earlier civilizations and with primitive societies, the threefolding in the tribal order works out in *instinctual* ways. In the modern epoch, intellectual development and the development of strong personalities (the self-will) bring about some helpful influences but also some very harmful influences. Individual development—a person being something like an island unto himself (unimaginable in the earlier tribal cultures)—tends to bring about a situation where a person can be "right" from his/her own personal perspective but can fail completely to appreciate the life of the community and the greater whole.

Some archetypal polarities emerge:

The Individual........................... The Whole Society
Personal good........................... Good of the whole
Individual perspective............... The threefold whole
Projecting the part.................... Perceiving the whole
Personality............................... Soul
Individual right.......................... Group good

The question is: When is a society healthy? When an individual has the opportunity to develop his/her full potential, without interfering in the right development of other individuals. The same can be said of the social domains as a whole. A society is healthy when each domain is able to have full opportunity for development, reaching its full potential, without interfering in the right development of other social domains.

According to Rudolf Steiner:

*Heilsam ist nur, wenn*
*Im Spiegel der Menschenseele*
*Sich bildet die ganze Gemeinschaft*
*Und in der Gemeinschaft*
*Lebet der Einzelseele Kraft.*

(Well being exists only
When in the mirror of the human soul
The whole community is reflected
And when there lives in the community
The strength of each individual soul.)

**Inevitable Bias.** It is important, even crucial, to understand that any given individual (particularly the *developed* individual) tends to identify with one or another of these three social domains. As personality scrambles to acquire, it also seeks to benefit (in an exclusive way) the particular domain with which it identifies.

Our personal bias is due primarily to two factors: *type* and *level*. Our personal prejudice is also complicated by what might be called the *illusion of knowing*. No one thinks that he is prejudice. Everyone thinks that he truly knows. As we view our own lives in retrospect, however, our own earlier misconceptions stand out clearly to the expanded, more mature view.

The factor of *level* has to do with age of personality, age of soul, chakra development, and degree of enlightenment. The "higher" or more refined the development, the more one is able to transcend personal prejudice and appreciate the whole.

The factor of *type* is related to the *seven rays* and to *esoteric astrology*. A strong 6th ray influence, for example, tends to bring one into the religious-spiritual approach to truth. Often this type, when relatively undeveloped and narrow, will have a marked prejudice against business and the Economic Sphere. This is true particularly when the 6th ray of idealism is modified by the 4th ray of beauty and art. This is not true when the 6th ray is modified by one of the more "concrete rays" (as opposed to ray of abstraction), such as the 1st ray of power, or the 3rd ray of intelligent activity.

58

An example of prejudice along the other line would be the following: A 1st ray and 3rd ray combination, particularly when the level of development is not refined, might have very little appreciation for the subtleties expressed in art and might think religion to be nothing more than a weakness and a delusion.

Each type tends to gravitate towards the social sphere with which there is compatibility and similarity of vibration. This is correct in that similarity of vibration facilitates the development of self. If we could refrain from pre-judging social spheres about which we have little knowledge, then we could approach a truer social order in which the major aspects functioned in right relationship, one with the other.

In the Middle Ages there was an ongoing and intense struggle-competition between Church and State. This took centuries to resolve. Nowadays, the interference and the struggle to survive exists between other social domains. The struggle between Business and State is especially intense at the present time. Being able to see the right relationship between the three major aspects is an arduous task that requires an appreciation of the whole, and an appreciation of triplicities—or how the whole manifests in a threefolding manner.

**Some Contemporary Examples of One Domain Interfering with Another**. Communism originally came about in the effort to correct some of the ills of capitalism—especially the *exploitation of labor*. Slaves had been emancipated and serfs were freed, but the industrial revolution managed to make economic slaves out of its workers. The machine operator was more expendable than the machine itself. Communism, however, went too far, and we had what was called the "dictatorship of the proletariat." Essentially what this was, was the State's interference in the Economic. A situation came about where there was, for all practical purposes, *no free enterprise*. We had State running business (State interfering with the Economic Domain) to the point of economic stagnation.

The Communist State also often interfered in the Spiritual-Cultural Domain. The State would only allow certain kinds of art. The State was anti-religious in many cases. The State oversaw education. On the positive side, the State provided education for many people who previously had had no opportunity to attend university, but also used education as a tool for State propaganda. Furthermore, the State did not do its own true work, which was to secure and protect human rights. Under communism the worker had many rights, such as the right to work (there was full employment) and the right to medical attention (everyone was covered under the State system). Many basic rights were lacking, however, such as freedom of the press, freedom of religion, freedom from unlawful searches, freedom to assemble, freedom to travel, etc.

In the West we have something like a reverse situation. In the West, particularly in the United States, *the Economic Domain is very strong, and this Domain seeks to influence and control the Government or the Rights-State Domain*. This can be seen only with the unbiased eye. There is a very intense battle going on between these two Domains at this time, and this conflict may take centuries to resolve. As Steiner puts it: "Priority must be given today to the all-important objective of working towards a *drastic separation of the economy from the rights-organization*" (*Towards Social Renewal* 70). In other words a separation of Business and State.

The call for election reform in the United States is a true call for the non-interference of business with government. *Environmental issues* are related to the issues of election reform and undue corporate influence. Business interests at times may want to exploit the natural resources beyond a point that is healthy for the environment. The question of what is a healthy environment, what constitutes a healthy forest, pure water, and clean air, etc., is a question that should be addressed to the spiritual-cultural realm. In other words, these questions should be referred to the scientific experts at the universities and to other technical experts. These are not questions to be decided in the economic sphere. The cultural sphere advises the legislature. The legislatures enact the necessary laws to safeguard a healthy environment. Certain limits would necessarily be placed on run-away economic growth and development. The right balance between natural resource use and over-use would be more quickly achieved if the focus were on quality of life, rather than quantity of goods.

According to Steiner: "Not the question: How can we bring law and culture more and more into dependence on the economic life? But rather: How can we escape from that dependence? That is the question to be asked before any other." (*The Social Future* 51.) When the economic sphere dominates the other two spheres (when people look to the economic to solve all their problems), then we have something similar—though in reverse—to the situation in which the government dominates the economic and cultural spheres under extreme socialism and communism. One sphere overpowers or over-influences the other two spheres to the point of inhibiting their right development.

Government regulation is often perceived as government interfering with business and free enterprise. Much of it, however, has to do with the question of rights. The government regulates automobile emissions because people have a *right to clean air*. Water pollution is regulated not only for endangered species, but also because people have a *right to clean water*. In the early part of the last century "snake oil" was sold, and there were many wondrous claims as to its healing properties. The Food and Drug Administration and truth-in-advertising laws address the important and fundamental rights dealing with labeling of ingredients and product testing.

**Democracy and the Right to Vote**. The Rights-Sphere at the present time is a democratic one, either in actuality, in goal, or in pressure from the people. That was not always the case. The Romans struggled with a token democratic Senate, but Rome was ruled by the dictates of an emperor. During the Middle Ages, an elite aristocracy came to power, and the Rights Domain developed an autocratic rule. The quest for a democratic style of government grew stronger during and after the Renaissance.

Childlike and uneducated humanity requires the autocratic rule of the dominant, parental person or group. As humanity grows and develops, the cry is for *equality before the law*, for the right to vote, the right to have a voice in how one is being governed. A higher form of government may yet evolve in the future where there are true initiate heads, true enlightened leaders, to help organize and guide the social organization of humankind.

It should be noted here that, according to Steiner, the Rights Domain is or should be a democratic one at this time. The other two spheres, however, are not democratic and cannot function in a democratic way. Whether or not a person is a great artist or a great plumber, has nothing to do with a democratic vote. The cultural or entrepreneurial leader is best identified by a group of experts, not by the man in the street.

*Government has to do with the factor of will and the first ray.* If a person is always controlled by someone else, by the parent, or by autocratic rule, then he or she will never develop fully as a human being. One could represent it in the following set of correspondences:

The Child.......... .immature......... autocratic rule...outside rule.

The Personality...individuality... democracy.........self rule.

The Soul.......group conscious.... unnamed............initiate rule

**Iran: A Contemporary Example of the Old Church and State Controversy**. Iran (Persia) began the 1900's with an autocratic government under the rule of a series of kings or shahs. Throughout the century there was a strong sentiment and will among the people of Iran towards a constitutional revolution and the forming of a democracy. In 1906, under the weak Qajar Dynasty, Persia's first constitution and first parliament were brought about. The constitution limited the power of the shah. The people's unrest and the quest for democracy had partly to do with the fact that the shah had given exclusive rights to tap Iran's oil to the British. *Here is a case, one of a great many, where a democratic colonial power supported, propped up, and sustained a non-democratic government in order to benefit themselves economically.* In other countries the same pattern was repeated in order to obtain at low cost oil, gold, diamonds, zinc, copper, nickel, coffee, bananas, and many other natural resources and economic products. The will behind these exploits and unfair trade arrangements was not the will of the State to secure democrat rights for its citizens. Rather it was the will of the Economic Sphere, misapplied, that was able to secure undue influence in the Domain of State. The State became an instrument of the Economic will.

In 1953 the last Pahlavi shah sought to dismiss his Prime Minister. The movement towards democracy was gaining momentum and threatening the survival of the autocratic rule by the shah. The effort backfired on him, however, and the shah fled to Rome. By this time the United States also had keen economic interests in Iran. The C.I.A. and British Intelligence were able to orchestrate riots in Tehran and force the Prime Minister Mossadeq to resign. *They helped to re-establish the non-democratic rule of the shah for another 25 years.* The Economic Sphere, influencing the Rights-State or government of democratic nations, was able to prevent the will of the people and a true democratic state from coming about.

Eventually the rule of the shah was overturned (1979) The Ayatollah Khomeini, who had been in exile in France, held up the hope of democracy for the people. At first, the Ayatollah said that the *religious leaders should not administer the state.* He said that government should be run according to Islamic laws (the Sharia), but *he did not advocate cleric rule.*

**Old Problems of Church Interfering in State Re-Surfaced**. The sixth ray of idealism must be one of the rays conditioning the state of Iran, for they were not able to stay away from the fiery interference of the clerics in matters of state. (The 6th ray of idealism and devotion is also one of the rays conditioning the Islamic religion.) What emerged, not immediately but within a few years, was a theocracy. *Old questions about the need for the separation of Church and State re-surfaced.*

In the new republic the president had little more than a title. Most of the power was invested in the Velayat-e Faqih or Supreme Ruler. This is comparable to a political papacy, similar to the time when the pope directly ruled that portion of Italy known as the Papal States. There are three branches of government in the new system—executive, judicial, and legislative—but each branch has a "shadow" position or institution (made up of clerics) with equal or more power. For example, the Parliament has 270 members. There is also a 12 member Council of Guardians which has veto power over laws enacted by Parliament, if the laws are deemed un-Islamic.

One has to realize that part of the fanatic religious-cultural purity that some of the present day Islamic States insist upon, has to do with a fear of being corrupted by the many blatant impurities of Western culture. If one looks at both cultures with an unprejudiced eye (something that is extremely difficult to do), one will see that both are right and both are wrong. A lack of freedom in the arts, culture, and religion is not healthy for a society. The Spiritual-Cultural Domain requires liberté or freedom. The State needs to consider all matters dealing with individual rights and freedoms. On the other hand, when business interests dominate the arts, then art becomes prostituted and does not develop its intrinsic worth and contribution. This results in an unhealthy culture and often a sick society.

One of the major difficulties confronting humanity at the present time has to do with the fact that we are in a transition time between Ages. The 6th Ray of the Piscean Age is waning, and the 7th Ray of Organization and Ceremonial Magic of the Aquarian Age is on the increase. That will completely alter our civilizations at a fundamental level and in a comprehensive way.

**Business and Culture**. Related to the above is the matter of the relationship between the Economic Domain and the Spiritual-Cultural Domain. In Europe, the cultural situation seems to have far deeper roots and far deeper traditions than is true in the United States. The "pop" culture of the United States has to do with popularity, which means, box office proceeds, the number of books sold, the number of compact discs sold, the number of people viewing the television program, etc. Appealing to the quantitative factor and to the lowest common denominator, we have a huge multi-billion dollar entertainment industry run by business for financial gain. The Economic Sphere intrudes deeply into the Cultural Domain, and many an artist feels that he/she must sell his/her soul in order to survive. Some, however, choose to maintain their art as a cultural phenomenon, preserved outside of the controlling influence of those who place a priority on quantitative factors.

In the Spiritual-Cultural realm the alignment with the "jealous" Muse (the spiritual influence) is just about everything. It is close to everything when it comes to true creativity—a creativity that has an edifying and uplifting effect on struggling humanity. *Culture is meant primarily to inspire, to educate, to heal, and to edify. It is meant to be revelatory in terms of revealing the meaning of life.* It is meant to address and answer in part the Big Questions. It is not meant to make money. It is not meant to create a product that sells well. That is incidental to the larger purpose. It is not meant to make someone rich and famous. It wasn't too long ago when culture enjoyed a more spiritual and edifying status. But with the tremendous growth in the economic sector, there have been many new opportunities presented (beneficial ones, like technological advancements), but there has also been an eclipsing of some of the deepest cultural values.

What about the cultural scene in Iran? When the shah was in power, his cooperation with the Western powers brought some Western cultural influences. The clerics deemed these, for the most part, corrupting. When the shah was displaced, the theocracy established their own form of censorship. Western influences were eliminated almost altogether, and a new Iranian culture was encouraged (to a degree). At first only narrow propaganda films were allowed to be made. Hardly anyone went to see them. Then the Ayatollah Khomeini encouraged artistic films, and this enabled some film makers to grow and develop in their art form. This brought about significant changes in the Iranian film world. The Iranian film director Mehrjui said: "The whole world of cinema during the past twenty years has been engulfed and devoured by commercial cinema. More and more, the grand tradition of making films as art, especially in Europe, Latin America and India, has died out because of the domination of American cinema. Iran is the only country that still has a tremendous enthusiasm for deep, existential, artistic films that are truthful about life—because our doors are locked to American and other commercial films. So our cinema is not only alive, it's flourishing." (Robin Wright, *The Last Great Revolution: Turmoil and Transformation in Iran*, 129.)

Surprise, surprise! Yet there are problems. One of his films was not officially banned, but the ministry shelved it for seven years. In making a film he had to be very careful to be politically (and religiously) correct and not to offend anyone.

The question is: Who makes the decision as to which films will be produced and which ones will not? In the West it might be a corporate head or a department head whose primary concern is how much will the film gross. In a theocracy like Iran, it might be a government ministry made up of clerics who judge the work along dogmatic religious lines. In the first case artistic integrity is lost to business interests and the market plane. In the second instance artistic freedom is inhibited by a narrow theological doctrine. In the first case the Economic Sphere interferes with the Cultural Domain. In the second instance, the religious part of the Cultural Domain working through the Rights State interferes with the artistic aspect of the Cultural Domain. In both cases one either has "bad" art, kitsch, or an art that struggles to find a voice within the narrow confines of formulas and prescribed patterns.

Who should make the decisions as to what art is produced? According to Steiner, each of the social spheres needs to be self-administered (*Renewal* 78). Imagine, for a moment, something like a university publishing house. Generally speaking, these subsidized publishing houses are cultural events first and business operations a far second, if at all. The obligation of the university is, generally speaking, to further the culture. There are many other cultural administrated bodies whose primary purpose is to further one of the arts, such as a great opera house. There are always financial concerns—source of money can be contributions, endowments, fees, government subsidies—but the people making the key decisions are those who have expertise in the particular cultural field.

The same principle applies to the other social spheres. One would not want an essentially government minded person making business decisions (as was the case in the Soviet Union). Nor would one want business decisions being made on religious grounds. Sometimes it is very clear as to which domain the decision belongs, and sometimes, particularly in this era of pronounced personality development and bias, it is not clear at all.

66

One thinks that the system is too monolithic and too entrenched to change. Yet as new ideas are intuited, change proceeds. Nothing is static. Change happens all the time. New forms have to be created in order to house the expanding spirit. When consciousness grows, we wake up to how imprisoning our social order is. When the principle is understood, then the new forms can be created.

Needless to say, we have hardly scratched the surface of this important topic. At this point, however, that is all that we have time to do. We bring it forth simply as a means of suggesting how the seven ray energies interweave in the environment and how knowledge of the seven rays can help tremendously to understand the world in which we live.

> Our little systems have their day;
> They have their day and cease to be:
> They are but broken lights of thee,
> And thou, O Lord, art more than they.

From *In Memoriam*, by Alfred Lord Tennyson

# The THREE RAYS OF ASPECT and THREE PRACTICAL KEYNOTES: EMPOWERMENT, APPRECIATION, and CLARIFICATION

**The Three Keynotes**. When relating and working with other people, the keynotes of *empowering* others, *appreciating* others, and *clarifying* the whole of matters with others, help us to use the ray energies in an intensely practical way.

These three—*empowering, appreciating, and clarifying*—are especially beneficial when there is any kind of authority-power relationship involved. This would include:

parent to child
employer to employee
manager to worker
supervisor to direct server
therapist to client
counselor to friend
teacher to pupil
coach to player
director to actor etc., etc.

Behind these three keynotes stand the three energies of the rays of aspect. Working with them would help to approximate a more holistic perspective.

Endeavoring to embody these energies would help to move from personality limitation and self-centeredness to soul attitude and responsibility. These three keynotes are in some respects the antithesis of personality. *They constitute the way we would like to be treated, but not the way we generally treat others.* We seek to empower ourselves, but we like it when someone empowers us. We usually ask others to appreciate our point of view or our work, but we are very reluctant to express appreciation for the work of a friend or colleague. We spend effort to clarify our point of view, but seldom do we find the person who can clarify the whole of the situation.

68

**Empowering Others**. There are always paradoxes when it comes to the differences between soul and personality. When you empower others, when you strengthen others, it may appear to some that you are giving your power away, but in reality you yourself are also strengthened. But this is almost a non-relevant by-product. From the group conscious soul this is completely incidental.

Self-empowerment tends to use *force* and to result in the loneliness of standing isolated from others. Empowering others tends to use *energy*—the connection with the divine circulatory flow—and brings one into the true group of brotherhood. The reality of the One Work then replaces the illusion of "my work."

When we work to empower ourselves, we are actually working in the direction of form-materialism, which has its limitations and runs its course. Empowering the good in others, connects one in consciousness with what has true continuity.

D.K.'s statement to R.R.R. in the book *Discipleship in the New Age* relates to our theme. "You are needed in the work and have much to give. You have strength and can strengthen others when your own strength is deflected away from yourself and your dramatic sense of self-pity. You have great wisdom and can use it, once you lose sight of yourself as a teacher." DNA, v.1, 658.

**Appreciating Others**. Appreciating others brings in an entirely different energy, though it is also related to strengthening. When we empower others, we look to see how we can strengthen their position-situation, and also how we can strengthen them physically, emotionally, and mentally.

*The factor of appreciation carries a 2nd ray energy.* It speaks to the warmth of heart and soul. There is a tendency for one to favor either the 1st ray energy of empowerment or the 2nd ray energy of appreciation. Many people who deal with power on a daily basis almost never express an appreciation for others. In our effort here to understand the importance of *the whole* and the importance of the *basic triplicity*, this prejudicial leaning one way or the other needs to be most carefully noted. One way will always be a path of least resistance, due to one's own psychological ray make-up. One will always have to give much thought and effort to move forward in a more holistic fashion.

Appreciation also brings love and understanding. How many people go through life feeling a certain hurt simply because a key person—say, a parent or an employer or even a spouse—never expressed a word of appreciation. When one's work and effort goes unappreciated, the whole group suffers and its effectiveness is diminished.

Appreciation touches the quality factor and goes from heart-to-heart. When we express appreciation, we must be able to see that invisible and valuable *qualitative something* that a person offers to the group and to the life around. Due to the competitive tendency of personality, this is not easily apprehended. The subtle contribution of another is often best discerned in quiet reflective meditation.

In a letter to R.S.U., the following suggests were given by D.K.:

The meditation I would give you is based on the words "as a man thinketh in his heart, so is he." I would have you, therefore, think out with care the differences that would appear in your personality expression if you had a second ray astral body. I will also set you the task of writing out for me, my brother, a paper in which you will emphasize the characteristics of a second ray astral body. You will then endeavor each day to build in these second ray qualities. They are built in through the *second ray methods of love, contact, attraction, understanding, sympathy and compassion*. The latter two qualities are almost totally lacking in your equipment and your career as an executive director has necessarily enhanced this defect. I would remind you that I did not say that you lacked love. You used, in the past, to supplement this defect by *an intuitive appreciation of people* but lately you have hardened in one direction—that of sympathy—and crystallized into a racial pattern which is not yours; it is based on the development of the heart centre which has, as yet, only opened in the direction of your own people and towards Masonry. (*Discipleship in the New Age*. v.1, 374)

R.S.U. had the following ray equipment:

```
Soul.................2nd ray
Personality.........3rd ray
    mental body............1st ray
    astral body..............1st ray
    physical body..........7th ray
```

The 1st ray astral body is contrary to the usual pattern of having either a 2nd ray astral or a 6th ray astral body.

The 1-3-7 energy gives this person something of an imbalance along the tougher ray line of will, intelligence, and organization. She was a Capricorn lawyer and social worker, and, as indicated above, a woman of considerable executive ability. The ambitious Capricorn goat is often able to painstakingly and methodically climb to the top of one's profession.

The need here is to balance the 1-3-7 energy with the 2nd ray love-wisdom energy of the soul. As mentioned above, usually the astral body is on either the 2nd or 6th rays. Had any one of the personality vehicles or bodies been on the 2-4-6 line (such as a 4th ray mind, or a 6th ray astral body), then that would have been the vehicle through which or by means of which the soul energy could have been brought into play. But such was not the case. There was no personality aspect or body through which the soul could come easily into play.

The suggestion given to R.S.U. by the Tibetan teacher, D.K., was to work on changing the note of the astral body from the 1st ray to the 2nd ray—no easy or quickly achieved task but one she was capable of accomplishing.

The meditative use of *keywords*, embodying qualities or *qualitative energy*, is a method used to bring about balance, wholeness, and soul unfoldment. The keywords suggested here are: *love, contact, attraction, understanding, sympathy, compassion, and appreciation.*

**Clarifying the Whole.** This requires the third aspect of *intelligence.* What is helpful here is an holistic paradigm, such as the seven rays provide. Esoteric astrology also enables one to appreciate the whole of things.

When two people have polarizing points of view, almost always they are both correct, from each individual perspective, but they are also wrong, for they fail to see the validity in the opposing point of view—and they fail to see the whole. The more they oppose each other, the more they try to fortify their own perspective and find the flaws in the opponent's perspective. The more developed and wiser one must be able to make the effort to see and understand the opposing point of view. The illusion is that we know, but what we know is only a part, a fragment. Effort must be made to recognize the validity of all perspectives. One must see and *be able to clarify* the other point of view.

D.K. mentions that one of the requirements of aspirants today is "the clarifying of the mental life in the pure light of the soul. Disciples live too much in the world of feeling; hence the clouding of their vision. When they have clarified their minds and see the situation whole, they can then appeal to the Avatar to make His appearance. This appeal must be made via the Christ." (*Externalization of the Hierarchy*, 311)

One of the factors that work against the process of intelligently clarifying issues is related to the degree of emotionalism involved. The emotionalism, or "world of feeling", is related to one's personal desire life. Basically, we want something for ourselves, and this clouds the vision, or prevents the person from approaching a more holistic perspective. Our personal desire or ambition creates a veil between us and the other point of view. It is necessary to detach and release ourselves from our own perspective. When progress has been made in that direction, then we can call upon the higher unifying principle—the soul, the Christ aspect—in order that the holistic resolution is recognized or intuited.

**In Summary**, one way to think about the three major ray energies of Will, Love, and Light, is in the practical triplicity of

1. *Empowering* others, strengthening others. Making others more self-reliant. Sharing responsibility.
2. *Appreciating* others. Relating heart-to-heart. Meditatively reflecting on the helpful and invisible contribution of others.
3. *Clarifying* the other point of view in the effort to intuit the larger, the relative, and the transcendent whole.

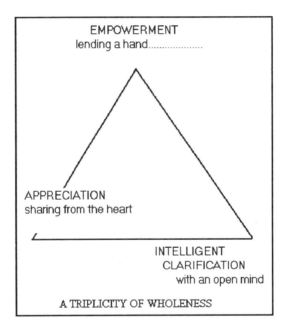

EMPOWERMENT
lending a hand.....................

APPRECIATION
sharing from the heart

INTELLIGENT
CLARIFICATION
with an open mind

A TRIPLICITY OF WHOLENESS

(See: *Techniques of Soul Alignment: The Rays, the Subtle Bodies, and the Use of KEYWORDS* for an in-depth look at how keywords are used.)

73

# The SEVENTH RAY as
# LIVING CATHEDRAL

From a certain perspective the seventh ray is perhaps the most "visible" of the seven qualifying ray energies in that it is one of the four rays of attribute, and it is also the ray that conditions most strongly the physical-etheric plane. From another perspective, however, the seventh ray is the ray of the incoming Aquarian Age, and from that angle this energy is relatively new to us. In many ways we are far more familiar with the sixth ray quality of idealism and devotion (as it conditioned the Piscean Age) than we are with the quality of organization, relationship, and ceremonial magic. How are we to know the seventh ray energy in a practical and living sense?

**Cathedral as Symbol of Unity**. James Parks Morton, Dean of the Cathedral of St. John the Divine in New York, is involved in a movement that begins with a redefinition of the word "cathedral." According to Morton, the connotation that cathedral has in the minds of most Americans is "historical monument" and "medieval, authoritarian Europe." Cathedral as he sees it, however, is something else altogether. It is "urban, represents all of life; it's artistic, it's political, it's economic, it's social, it's sociological—all of these dimensions." He points out that the cathedral was always on the market place and that it was a sort of "summation and culmination of all that was in the city.... A cathedral was the symbol of what unites all." It is *not* a "communion of identicals," rather it is a "communion of differences." (*Lorian Journal,* vol. III, no. 2.)

In Morton's redefinition of cathedral it can be noted that he is moving away from the concept—if not strongly opposed to the concept—of authoritative religion and religion as an endeavor that stands opposed to other facets of society. He sees "cathedral" as something that represents or unifies or synthesizes all of life—the political as well as the religious, the economic and social as well as the artistic.

74

From a qualitative angle, what is Morton actually trying to identify? Tentatively, let us suggest that what is occurring here is a repulsion of the sixth ray of idealism and devotion (as a dominant vibration) in an effort to articulate and manifest the quality of the synthesizing seventh ray of organization and ceremonial magic. Consider the following brief list of stated and implied concepts associated with these two ray energies as suggested by Morton's struggle:

OUTGOING 6th RAY               INCOMING 7th RAY
Separative, selective...................Unifying
One-pointedness........................Diversity
Communion of identicals............Communion of differences
Isolated..................................... Urban
Authoritarian............................ Cooperative
Religious................................... Religious, political, artistic,
                                                        economic, sociological

**Craftsmanship and Ritualized Modes of Behavior.**  Another important quality of "cathedral" deals with *craftsmanship* or "modes of behavior that are stereotyped or ritualized."  In craftsmanship Morton emphasizes the "correct way" rather than the individually unique way of doing something.  He uses the example of handwriting to the point of illegibility. "It is the same way with someone who is chopping stone in our cathedral stoneyard, where the master builder won't allow people to do it incorrectly.  There is a way in which your personality and that which is uniquely you, your signature, will come out in that stone, but that comes out through your having mastered something that would appear at first to be almost an obliteration of your uniqueness.  You first have to cut the stone—get it absolutely correct—and then on top of that your personality or uniqueness is very obvious."

In social interaction there are also "stereotyped or ritualized" modes of behavior.  Civility he defines as "the way you behave in a city."  In some countries you shake hands with your right hand, drive on the right side of the road, stop at red lights, dress for certain occasions in a certain way, etc. It is not a matter of good or bad, but a matter of correct or incorrect. There are such things as manners, which are "purely structural things in social intercourse." They have to with the crafting of human relationship. from the behavior and form side, and can be seen as something of an art form. "It is not casual; it is very defined; it is this way and not that way. But that is what builds up a neighborhood or a family or a city; these are rituals of living."

In contrast to civility and ritualized modes of behavior, Morton recalls an extreme situation in the 1960's when some people would not shake hands with someone of they did not like the person. "To me that is the absolute breakdown of civilization, when people 'interiorize' and say that they are not going to behave unless they can make personal value judgments on that person." The quality of being an individual generally has a positive connotation in contemporary Western society. Morton is suggesting, however, that this quality can be carried to an extreme, resulting in a breakdown in relationship and communication. People can become so highly individualized that a lack of civility can occur.

In Alice Bailey's *Esoteric Psychology* we find that one of the effects of the 6ixth ray has been the fostering of the "sense of separativeness and of pronounced individualism." "The sixth ray promoted the growth of the spirit of individualism. Groups exist, but they are groups of individuals gathered around an individual. The seventh ray will foster the group spirit, and the rhythm of the group, the objective of the group, and the ritual-working of the group will be the basic phenomena.... The seventh ray will...emphasize unity but bar out uniformity." (*Esoteric Psychology*, v.1, 366, 361, 362.)

| SIXTH RAY | SEVENTH RAY |
|---|---|
| sense of separativeness | unity, not uniformity |
| pronounced individualism | group spirit |
| unpredictable individuality | civility, ritual |
| casual behavior | defined behavior |
| individually unique artist | master craftsman |

**Relating Spirit and Matter**. "The Communion, the Eucharist, the Mass," according to Morton, "is central to Christian living precisely because it is the continual process of incarnation, of the Spirit taking and filling and transforming flesh, matter, stuff—making it perfect. There is a tendency within all kinds of spiritualities of going spiritual at the expense of the flesh. In the West, it is most typical in neo-Platonism, where the body is essentially despised, a prison, and when you are trying to rescue the pure Spirit from the body." Rev. Morton would have us not neglect, ignore or despise the form, rather he would have us work with the Spirit in the process of filling and perfecting the form. Despising the flesh does not enable us to resurrect it. "What the Mass is,... is the eternal resurrection of bread and wine, which again, is manufactured stuff. I mean it has human sweat in it."

Taking matter and making it perfect is related to art, to our physical bodies, and also to the "body politic and our cities and architecture. I can't just throw my body out the window and expect a new one. I can't throw my city out the window and expect a new one. I've got to massage that city and paint it and wash it and exercise it.... What a cathedral does is keep the fundamental artisans of the body politic at their top form—because the cathedral has the best stone cutters, the best glass people, the best dancers, singers, actors, scientists, biologists, politicians. All of them consecrate their work at the highest level."

Can we see the seven rays functioning here? Is there anything new or particularly significant in Morton's view? Can we gain an historical perspective and see trends that extend far beyond our little individual lives?

In *Esoteric Psychology* we find several references to the seventh ray's work of *relating spirit and matter* in a vital and living way. "The work of the Ray of Ceremonial Order is to 'ground' or make physically visible the results of bringing spirit and matter together. Its function is to clothe spirit with matter producing form." "The task of the new age worker is to bring these two apparent opposites together, to demonstrate that spirit and matter are not antagonistic to each other and that throughout the universe there is only spiritual substance, working on and producing the other tangible forms" (*Destiny of Nations*, 46, 127).

From one perspective, the sixth ray of idealism has prepared the way for the seventh ray's task of relating spirit and form in that it has "fostered the vision. The seventh ray will materialize that vision" (*Esoteric Psychology*, i, 359).

But why the antagonism? Why cannot there be a smooth transition from the preparatory work of the sixth ray to the more practical, form-producing work of the seventh ray? Due to this importance of the following statement, we quote it at length:

> The sixth ray devotee is far more abstract and mystical in his work and thought, and seldom has any real understanding of the right relationship between form and energy. He thinks almost entirely in terms of quality and pays little attention to the material side of life and the true significance of substance as it produces phenomena. He is apt to regard matter as evil in nature and form as a limitation, and only lays emphasis upon soul consciousness as of true importance. It is this failure to work intelligently, and I would like to add, lovingly with substance and so bring it into right relationship with the dense outer form that has made the last two thousand years produce so disastrously a mismanaged world and which has brought the population of the planet into its present serious condition. The unintelligent work upon the physical plane, carried forward by those influenced by the sixth ray force, has led to a world which is suffering from cleavage in as true a sense as an individual person can suffer from a split personality. The lines of demarcation between science and religion are a striking instance of this and have been clearly and forcefully drawn.
>
> *Destiny of Nations*, 127.

Identifying the polarities helps us gain clarity on the issues:

| SIXTH RAY | SEVENTH RAY |
|---|---|
| desiring pure spirit | relating spirit and matter |
| fostering the vision | materializing the vision |
| abstract | concrete |
| mystical | practical |
| quality | substance |
| mismanagement | intelligent management |
| religion and science separate | relates religion and science |
| ignoring the form | perfecting the form |
| despising the flesh | transforming flesh with spirit |

78

If the teaching on the seven rays is an accurate one (and no one is being asked to accept this teaching blindly and devotionally), then Rev. Morton's concept of "cathedral" seems to be profoundly in step with the changing times. Surely his own psychological ray equipment helps him to attune to the incoming seventh ray energy. The use of the specific word "cathedral", as symbol of the incoming seventh ray energy, seems to be confirmed in the following quote from *Esoteric Psychology*: "What can now be seen in the organization of a crystal, a jewel and a diamond, with their beauty of form and line and color, their radiance and geometrical perfection, will appear likewise through the medium of the universe as a whole. The Grand Geometrician of the universe works through the seventh ray, and thus sets His seal upon all form life, particularly the mineral world. This the Masonic Fraternity has always known, and this concept it has perpetuated symbolically in the great world cathedrals, which embody the glory of the mineral world and are the sign of the world of the Master Builder of the universe" (*Esoteric Psychology*, i, 373).

# Other Examples of Seventh Ray Energy

**Belief Versus Knowledge.** *Realizing that we are dealing with hints and suggestions of what may later be great and far-reaching changes in our institutions and our way of life, what other examples of the seventh ray can be noted?*

"Belief in the soul has become widespread during the sixth ray period. Knowledge of the soul will be the result of the incoming ray activity" (*Esoteric Psychology*. v.i, 364)

We have two keywords here: One is *belief* (sixth ray) and the other is *knowledge* (seventh ray). Belief deals with an emotional sensing, a feeling, an envisioning (vitally important factors, to be sure); knowledge deals with mental clarity and practical application—the type of knowledge that is not merely intellectual but rather knowledge that is filled with experience and a relative wholeness. The question nowadays is less "Do you *believe* in God, in reincarnation, in science, in evolution, etc.?" The question is more: What do you actually *know* of these subject matters? What had been your direct experience with these matters. Not what you conceptually think is true, but what you embody with your whole being.

In the Middle Ages belief was paramount. Now one is certainly entitled to his/her opinion, but if one does not have study, research, and experience to back up the opinion—that is to say, *knowledge*—then one's opinion is, at best, politely indulged but of little consequence. The clear mental point of relative whole or complete knowledge holds more power and influence than does the personal belief. But it must be remembered, as we pursue knowledge of the seven rays, that each ray is a stupendously great life or being—an aspect of Deity. Belief still plays a major role in the development of consciousness. Each ray energy, each Being, forms a vitally important aspect of a celestially orchestrated whole. As the ray energies cycle in and out of manifestation, however, at any given time (within the space-time dimension) the work of one ray may appear to be of more relative importance than the work of another.

80

**Patriotism Versus Internationalism.** "The effect of the sixth ray has been to foster the separate instincts, dogmatic religion, scientific factual accuracy, schools of thought with their doctrinal barriers and exclusiveness, and the cult of patriotism. The seventh ray will...emphasize unity but bar out uniformity, and it will prepare for that internationalism which will express itself as practical brotherhood and as peace and goodwill between the people" (*Esoteric Psychology*, i, 362).

In religion we find the separative aspect of the sixth ray expressed as a blind devotion to a particular belief system, accompanied often by the thought that one's own religious belief system is the only true one. The others are viewed as either erroneous or devoid of any true merit—they are supposedly filled with "false doctrine."

In government and politics, along with the first ray of power, we also find the presence of the sixth ray of idealism. "As I told you, and as I now repeat, the workers on all the rays are organized to take part in one supreme effort,—an effort towards which the entire Christian era has been tending and for which it has been a preparation. The seventh and sixth rays are occupied with the work of government and with the task of producing a new synthesis, and thus the force of all the workers along those lines is combining with the energy of the first ray." (Eso. Psych, i, 178.) The sixth ray plays a major role in the political arena, as each party or faction works towards ideal social forms. As the sixth ray wanes and the seventh ray increases in power and influence, some of the negative excesses of the sixth ray (placing belief above evidence, the narrow definition, the black-white terms, the fanatical adherence, etc.) will steadily recede.

Patriotism is necessary in order to evolve a national identity. Youth is often filled with patriotic zeal. This is the same sort of energy that cheers dramatically for a particular team in a sporting event. But patriotism becomes blind to principle when it says "My nation, right or wrong." On principle, the question of right or wrong takes precedence over one's own nation. There are multiple nations, multiple races, but there is one humanity, and everyone belongs to that one family of nations and people. The seventh ray

81

brings in a unity with diversity. The seventh ray will help to organize differences into a beautiful mosaic where each part makes its unique contribution to the good of the whole.

The movement towards *unity, internationalism, sharing, and brotherhood* are also related to the work of Master M.—"inspirer of the great national executives throughout the world" (*Externalization of the Hierarchy* 505)—and also to "a very real measure of monadic energy" (*Discipleship in the New Age*, ii, 269). Nowadays, when a politician proudly talks about "the national interest," it is almost an embarrassment. One immediately wonders about the adverse effect the particular measure or position may have upon other nations and on the good of the whole.

Those who tend to misunderstand the very real tendency towards internationalism and the true meaning of brotherhood need our patience. The *uniqueness of the individual, diversity* (not uniformity), and *freedom* are all very essential new age qualities. Those movements or programs or organizations that seek to compromise the fundamental values of freedom and diversity are not true new age values.

**Group Work.** "First: Let it be constantly remembered that the new discipleship is primarily an experiment in group work and that its main objective is not the perfecting of the individual disciple in the group." (*Discipleship in the New Age*, i. 8.) At the beginning of the Aquarian Age we are beginning to see many *experiments in group work.* Everywhere things are subtly changing. Changes happen so subtly and gradually that one either has to have the perspective of a whole lifetime in order to get some feeling for the changes that have occurred, or one has to be a careful student of history—the kind of student that tries to see the consciousness of the earlier periods, as well as the different forms.

The development of a great many "self-help" groups is one possible indication of the emergence of a new group spirit. Self-help groups nowadays address a multitude of problems. There are victims of crime groups, single mother groups, abused children groups, over-eaters groups, parents of teenagers who have committed suicide groups, drug and alcohol groups, people suffering from a particular disease support groups, anger management groups, etc. The list is very long.

Perhaps one of the reasons why the self-help groups are so successful is that in many cases the suffering is so intense and the need so acute that personalities drop their usual barriers, which allows the group-conscious soul energy to enter, to circulate, and to heal. Also, when people come together with a similar problem, a certain mutual understanding enables the heart energy (the love of the soul) to enter and to elevate the group. Another interesting factor in regard to these groups is that there is no sense of separativeness vis-à-vis other groups. This is in contrast to church groups, for example, that may cultivate a certain amount of cohesiveness among themselves, yet often stand in separative superiority to other groups.

Another most significant factor among the self-help groups is that they are not dependent upon a leader. People come and go, but the group remains a vital and cohesive unit. There is leadership by the group rather than by any particular individual.

Another key factor in many self-help groups has to do with their ability to reach a practical spirituality without any particular religious belief system. They may mention Spirit, or Higher Power, or God, and they may very well experience some aspect of Deity as a living phenomenon, but there is no need to make Scholastic-like differentiations as to what this might mean. The self-help-group experience brings in a heart-felt spiritual energy that is both supportive and practical. As such, it seems very close to the seventh ray of organization and ceremonial magic.

**Business Organizations**. Certain changes in business groups might also suggest the incoming influence of the seventh ray. Dr. Jard DeVille is a psychologist whose area of special interest is the corporate world, as we have seen in an earlier chapter. He suggests to managers and corporate leaders that they strive for smallness in relationship rather than largeness. He advocates what he call "performance teams" and "growth centers" within the organization, rather than a large headquarters group in a distant location. He also advocates drawing a large number of employees into the decision-making process. He feels that an organization should consider not only monetary rewards but psychological and spiritual rewards as well. He feels that employees should deal with each other as much as possible, rather than through several tiers of managers.

It seems that a significant factor in the new groups has to do with the vital participation of every person in the group. Machinery increases to take the place of non-thinking slave-type labor. The dignity of the individual, at whatever level, will find its recognition in the New Age. The Old Age was terribly mismanaged from several perspectives.

**Dee Hock's Chaordic Age.** Dee Hock (founder and CEO Emeritus of VISA International) has recently written a book entitled *Birth of the Chaordic Age*. Dee Hock coined the word "chaordic", which is a joining of the two words Chaos and Order. This is Dee Hock's way of calling attention to the fact that our organizations cannot reduce everything (no matter how hard they try) to an absolutely controllable order. The effort to do so is a major part of the problem. "All things, even life itself, are a seamless blending of chaos and order." The questions that he has lived with and sought to answer through his long professional career are: *"Why are institutions, everywhere, whether political, commercial, or social, increasingly unable to manage their affairs? Why are individuals, everywhere, increasingly in conflict with and alienated from the institutions of which they are part? Why are society and the biosphere increasingly in disarray?"*

Throughout his career in banking, Dee Hock was confronted with organizations that seemed fundamentally flawed. He tried to figure out why. The Industrial Age developed a command-and-control style of management that has dominated the commercial, political, and social scene for the past 400 years. *The dominant command-and-control style is becoming increasingly irrelevant as organizations and societies worldwide become more diverse and more complex.* Organizations are failing, "not only in the sense of collapse, but in the more common and pernicious form—organizations are increasingly unable to achieve the purpose for which they were created, yet continuing to expand as they devour resources, decimate the earth, and demean humanity."

84

In spite of the obstacles of the present systems, Dee Hock was able to search for and to apply new principles of organization. He accomplished the impossible in his development of VISA International. He became one of only 30 living Laureates of the Business Hall of Fame. Yet his inner voice told him: "Business is not what your life is all about. Founding VISA and being its chief executive officer is something you must do, but it is only preparatory."

What are the reasons for organizational failure, and what can be done to develop new models of organization? When the perspective or paradigm is too linear, to mechanistic, too materialistic, then there is something like a disconnect from the "beautiful, magnificent flow of life." One retreats into little specialized departments, and one no longer affirms "the mystery of endless connectivity and wholeness." Life then loses meaning and content. People become whining and self-centered. Wining becomes the bottom line. People worship the gods of wealth, fame, and power. "It is a desperately sick society that does so; a society that turns its back on life and moves towards destruction and death. It is just such a society that we are creating."

In terms of the *knowledge* that a society might have, there is something like a natural movement from *data, to information, to knowledge*. First there is the experiencing of phenomena and the raw data. This develops into information as the data can be distilled into patterns and various units. This leads to knowledge about certain kinds of events, certain fields of experience, certain levels of information. *All this has been greatly enhanced in the scientific age.* There are also such factors, however, as *understanding and wisdom*, that have been more in the domain of the arts, philosophy, and religion. There has been an explosion in contemporary society's ability receive, utilize, generate, and send information. But there has become a "drowning of wisdom and understanding in a flood of data and information." Native societies were very wise. Our own society has less and less wisdom in proportion to the amount of information that it commands. "The result is a vast technological power unleashed with inadequate understanding of its systemic propensity for destruction."

The better type of organization (Dee calls it the "chaordic" organization) begins with *"Purpose,* then proceeds to *Principles, People* and *Concept,* and *only then* to *Structure* and *Practice."* Making money is not a Purpose. *Purpose* is related to *meaning.* Making money alone does not make one's life meaningful. One has to be able to say: If I work towards this particular Purpose, my life will be meaningful.

In Dee Hock's profound understanding of *organization,* it is necessary for the start-up people to spend much time together in the effort to understanding *Purpose.* In understanding the profundity of Purpose, one approaches an understanding of the "chaos" part (really the Spirit part) of "chaordic." The usual approach is to ignore spirit. This is done in ignorance, since it is utterly impossible to ignore the life that pervades everything. Dee Hock's approach is to approach life reverently. He recognizes that one cannot control the hand of spirit. To try to control spirit is to invite disaster. His effort is to include an approach to the influence and play of the spiritual aspects. *This seems to me to be very much related to the work of the seventh ray or organization and ceremonial magic.*

*Purpose, principle, and people are metaphorically akin to Heaven. Paper and procedure are more akin to Purgatory. Rules and regulations are Hell.* Rules, more often than not, have to do with the old style of ruling from the top down—a method that prevents creativity and trust. *"Rules and regulations, laws and contracts, can never replace clarity of shared purpose* and *clear, deeply held principles about conduct in pursuit of purpose."*

Dee Hock generally considers any organizational problem-situation from the angles of: 1) Where was it in the past, 2) How is it now, 3) What will it be in the future, and 4) How ought it to be? Dee Hock prefers to spend as much of the planning time as possible getting his associates to think together on *how things ought to be.* This helps them to get away from linear thinking, away from the illusion of believing one can control everything, and away from the selfish attitude. This enables the magic of community to break free to a new level of solution. Giving much thought to *how things ought to be* opens the mind to new spiritual solutions. These solutions, however, must find a practical way of becoming implemented. Once again, the seventh ray seem to resound loudly in these attitudes and procedures.

*What are healthy organizations?* According to Dee Hock, healthy organizations "induce behavior"—which is to say that they inspire behavior rather than "compel behavior." There is a destructive element to compelling or forcing behavior. Ideas and concepts such as hope, vision, meaning, values, and liberty play an integral part in the healthy organization. "When an organization loses its shared vision and principles, its sense of community, its meaning and values, it is already in the process of decay and dissolution, even though it may linger with the outward appearance of success for some time."

In his book *Birth of the Chaordic Age*, Dee Hock alternates between 1) the telling of the experiences he had while working with various corporations and 2) the discussion of the insightful concepts he had that grew out of his experience. He tells fascinating stories about working with VISA and other banking-finance organizations. His theorizing and his concepts are most helpful to others as they endeavor to make practical application of his experience. Many books these days take one or two points and stretch them into a mile. Dee Hock takes miles and years of intense struggle and condenses the experiences into jewels of knowledge and understanding. He does not waste the reader's time.

It seems that Dee Hock's soul compelled him to penetrate into the depths of the intrinsic nature of the institution. At several points in his life he could have eased into that common condition which he calls "retirement on the job." Since everything is controlled from the top down (command-and-control), one is forced into a sort of institutional straight-jacket. The younger, idealistic ones try at first to expand the "common sense and creativity" of the organization, but eventually they are forced to play the game of "predictability and control." Dee Hock reflected upon all the nonsense about being superior and inferior. There is no true measurement about the rightness of a direction, there is only the dictatorial pronouncements of those in controlling positions.

87

Instead of the top-down, control-command, model, all units within the organization—all indispensable in their own right—need to *self-organize in accordance with the Principles the organization espouses and around the Purpose that unites all.* In other words, instead of dictating rules and regulations, the managers are really enunciating principles around which other people gather. This is one of the new organizational factors that have a liberating effect.

In this regard also, it is important to realize that the Spirit cannot breathe into unprincipled organizations. Organizations of the future will be much more beautiful, much more purposeful, much more alive. It will be a joy to participate in them.

*The seventh ray worker* looks for the secret not in abstract heaven, but within the form itself. It looks for the true dynamic blending of spirit-form. The sixth ray Piscean Age rejected the earthly forms in so many ways. The result was a disconnect between spiritual endeavors and the business of survival. In the emerging Aquarian Age, the form—in this case the human institutions—must be alive with the spirit in them. We can no longer divide the world into an abstract distant spirit and a very immediate world of flesh, mammon, and profit. Humanity has to bring its organizational forms within the divine flow. Institutions (governmental, business, cultural-educational) cannot stand arrogantly out of the divine flow and threaten to destroy human dignity and the world in the process. Spirit, soul, meaning, wisdom, understanding are not pleasantries and niceties that stand outside of the real world of economic survival. The political, commercial, and social world cannot survive without wisdom and understanding.

**Another Example of the Seventh Ray Energy: The Findhorn Experiment.** The story of Findhorn reverberated around the world during the 70's and 80's. This little spiritual community in Scotland, started by Peter and Eileen Caddy, and Dorothy Mclean, sounded and continues to sound a very inspiring and profound seventh ray, New Age, note. Peter's book *In Perfect Timing* is a fascinating account of how he, along with others, was led to begin a truly unique community—a task to which he lent his own indomitable will.

In his developing years, he learned many managerial skills. Perhaps the most important had to do with working with a person's positive qualities, rather than pointing out the negative. When he was an apprentice hotel director, he noticed a young girl who did not seem to work well and who was being scapegoated by the other workers. He watched her closely for about a week until he finally found something that she did really well. He complemented her on her special skill. "She was so amazed and delighted that her attitude completely changed and she became one of the best workers in the establishment. From this experience I developed a practice of looking for the best in each person and acknowledging it with sincere praise. The dividends soon repaid the investment handsomely."

The old method has to do with criticizing the form and correcting the form. The new method has to do with recognizing the soul and spirit in the form and then letting the spirit from within correct the outer form. This is a task that seems more difficult at first, since it requires some patience and a new way of looking at things. In the long run, however, it is probably easier. It brings about true change, since change here is a result of growth and soul unfoldment.

**Manifesting One's Needs.** One of the important lessons that Peter had to learn early on was that he had to be very specific about his financial needs. After doing that he could place the matter completely in God's hands. Time and again the exact amount that he needed would come to him and often in unexpected ways. At one point Peter and Sheena needed to buy a more suitable car. This they did, but they had a lot of trouble selling their other car. Through Sheena's guidance they were told to come up with a specific amount in terms of their present financial needs and their unpaid bills. The amount was £375. Peter was quite worried about his unpaid bills, for he was getting court summonses and his career in the Royal Air Force was threatened. Finally, after he stopped worrying, which took about two weeks, and placed the matter completely in God's hands, *knowing that his needs would be met*, his car sold for exactly £375. This seems to be something that we probably could call a seventh ray phenomenon. 1) *There*

89

*is the need to be very specific about the material or financial requirement.* 2) Then there is the need to *trust in the spiritual life to meet the need or to bring two needs together.* 3) Then there is the need to *step aside and let Spirit do its work* in its own perfect sense of timing.

The seventh ray has to do with "magically" relating spirit and matter. It appears "magical" from the limited intellectual ability to comprehend these things, but from the spiritual point of view it really isn't magical at all. There is a subtler level of Law that is being followed. There are very specific things that must be recognized and followed. Also, spirit and matter *are related all the time.* The intellectual (linear) manner of cognizing often tends to focus on the densest aspects of the world of appearances and tends to deny evidence of the subtler aspects.

**Triangles of Energy**. Another interesting phenomenon that relates to the seventh ray has to do with a *network of triangles.* During his travels while still in the Royal Air Force, Peter met Naomi. "Her work had been to form a group of seven in Lexington Fields to contact, telepathically, groups of people all over the world, forming a 'Network of Light.' There were, within this group, both those who received and others who transmitted telepathically; in all, some 370 different groups had been contacted. The purpose of this Network of Light was to receive energies which were being poured down upon the planet. These energies were then transmitted and transformed, or stepped down, through a system of triangles from one level of power to anther—much as electricity in a national grid goes from one generating station to another, then to regional stations, local sub-stations, and finally fuse-boxes in buildings for individual use."

In the next 2000 the seventh ray energy will transform civilization as we know it today. We are not talking about a few minor adjustments here and there. We are talking about a world that will be as different from our world today as our world today is different from life on earth 2000 years ago. It is important to think of this change not only in terms of technological advancement, it is more important to think of it in terms of growth and expansion of consciousness.

We are given a clue as to the significance of "triangles of energy" in the book *Telepathy and the Etheric Vehicle*:

> I have said earlier that the intersecting energies in the etheric body of the planet are at this time a network of squares. When the creative process is complete and evolution has done its work, these squares will become a network of triangles. Necessarily this is a symbolic way of speaking. In the Book of Revelations which was dictated 1900 years ago by the disciple who is now known as the Master Hilarion, reference is made to the "city which stands four-square." The etheric vehicle of the planet was inherited from a former solar system, with the purpose or intention in view of its transformation into a network of triangles in this solar system. In the next one of the triplicity of solar systems (the third or last) in which the will of God works out, the etheric body will begin as a network of triangles, but this will be resolved into a network of interlinked circles or of linked rings, indicating the fulfillment of interlocking relationships. In this present system, the result of evolution, as far as the etheric body is concerned, will be the contact established between all three points of each triangle, making a ninefold contact and a ninefold flow of energy; this is consistent with the fact that nine is the number of initiation, and by the time the destined number of disciples have taken the nine possible initiations, this triangular formation of the planetary etheric body will be complete.
>
> *Telepathy and the Etheric Vehicle* 164.

From a certain angle one could think of the above energy patterns in the following way: *The Square* represents the energy pattern of *conflict* or *Fire by Friction*. In a certain sense this is akin to personality development. *The Triangle* represents a *blend* of energy, similar to the trine aspect in astrology. This is akin to *soul* and *Solar Fire*. The Circle represents synthesis and is akin to *Electric Fire*. From the sparks of friction, to the radiance of the soul energy, to the direct and dynamic connection to the Will of God. The New Age should see considerable progress towards unity, towards a profound recognition of the true spirit of brotherhood, which will alter the face of the earth.

91

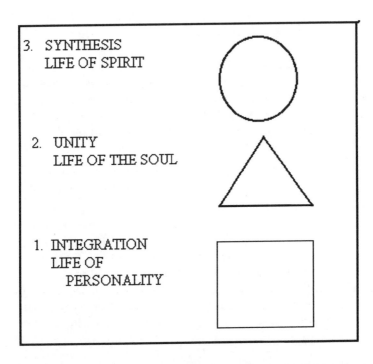

3. SYNTHESIS
   LIFE OF SPIRIT

2. UNITY
   LIFE OF THE SOUL

1. INTEGRATION
   LIFE OF
      PERSONALITY

**A Powerhouse of Love and Light**. When Peter left the Royal Air Force and got into the hotel business, his spiritual work continued to expand. Several of his co-workers were sensitives (including his wife Eileen). The sensitives always informed Peter of what was happening in the inner life of the employees and visitors, so that he could take appropriate action when there was a problem. "Cluny Hill quickly became a powerhouse of Love and Light, and we were told that hotels like it were to replace the monastic sanctuaries where people sought solace from the chaotic world. Those who came would leave refreshed in body and spirit, often without knowing why, but always hoping to come back."

As the Findhorn Community developed, a governing body known as the Core Group came into being. After a group meeting of argument and indecision, Eileen received the following guidance: *Why waste time and energy discussing and arguing about a problem and how to handle it? Why not be still and in the silence go within, and let Me reveal the truth to you? Never try to work out a solution with the mind. Let the mind be your servant, never the master. When you attune to Me, you each reach the same solution, for I am the universal mind. No problem is too small to bring to me. See the group functioning from the universal mind, and then everything will run smoothly, and there will be perfect harmony and oneness.*

The fifth root race prides itself on its intellectual abilities. Most all of us have experienced the frustration of spiritual groups using old age methods of intellectual discussion in order to solve problems. We are told that the Spiritual Hierarchy of the planet will sit in silence and wait for that inspiring point when all speak the same word simultaneously, as the solution drops in from the Higher Source. The above passage from Eileen's guidance gives us a feeling for how soul solutions to the problems of humanity can come about. Also, there is bridging work being done here towards the future 6th root race.

A strong will was required to help inaugurate a significant note of the seventh ray Aquarian Age energy in the Community at Findhorn. Peter's autobiography *In Perfect Timing* is a fascinating account of the life of a world disciple who accepted all presented challenges in the effort to further the Plan as he understood it and as it unfolded before his eyes on a day by day, moment by moment basis.

**Death, Leisure, and Population.** In Alice Bailey's book *Destiny of Nations* we find the following interesting statement:

> A large number of seventh ray egos or souls and also men and women with seventh ray personalities are coming into incarnation now, and to them is committed the task of organizing the activities of the new era and ending the old methods and the old crystallized attitudes to life, to death, to leisure, and to population.

*Destiny of Nations* 30.

That statement was written in 1949. In respect to death, it certainly seems that we have come a long way, although we still have very far to go. Attitudes towards dearth are slowly changing. Many cases of near-death-experiences have been recorded that present convincing evidence of life after death. Several reputable psychics are bringing messages to relatives from those on the other side. The well known work of Elizabeth Kubler-Ross has done much to give us a new perspective on the death experience. Instead of trying to ignore death, people are beginning to prepare more intelligently and lovingly for death. The hospice movement is developing and growing steadily.

New attitudes towards death are also new attitudes towards life. The view of materialistic science (not all science) that there is no life after death is being eroded by new evidence from several sources. New spiritual teaching, and also new clarification of ancient teaching, seems to be having a very pervasive and profound effect on our understanding of life-death. There is growing evidence that reincarnation is a fact. This includes the teaching of the Masters of Wisdom and also the clarification of initiates, such as Rudolf Steiner. Also, many are experiencing something from their earlier lives through past-life regressions.

The prediction is also that the seventh ray will profoundly affect our concept of leisure. The sixth ray suggests a polarity between intense, concentrated labor followed by rest or indulgence. Also, in the Old Age which is still with us in a great many ways, there is an unequal distribution of labor. Many work too much and many have no labor. Some stand on an elite economic pedestal while others work under conditions of virtual slavery. The seventh ray, on the other hand, suggests less of a polarity between work and leisure (unequal leisure and often unproductive leisure) and more of a rhythmic, organized system of complementary activities. When scientific advancements are rightly organized and equitably distributed, then there will be a great deal more leisure. Also with seventh ray knowledge, which brings the material in harmony with the spiritual, exploitation of people, the environment, the natural resources should come to an end. Natural resources and leisure are, of course, inextricably interwoven. One of the choices confronting us now has to do with the question of who controls the resources? To quote D.K.:

94

Money, the accumulation of financial assets and the cornering of the earth's resources for organizational exploitation will soon prove utterly useless and futile, provided that these resources of energy and the mode of their release remain in the hands of the people's chosen representatives and are not the secret possession of certain groups of powerful men or of any one nation. . . .

The problem of labor will then be the major problem of unemployment—a dreaded word which will be meaningless in the golden age which lies ahead. The masses will then be faced by the problem of leisure. This is a problem which when faced and solved will release the creative energy of man into channels undreamed of today. . .

The note to be struck and the word to be emphasized is humanity. Only one dominant concept can today save the world from a looming economic fight to the death, can prevent the uprising again of the materialistic systems of the past, can stop the re-emerging of the old ideas and concepts and can bring to an end the subtle control by the financial interests and the violent discontent of the masses. A belief in human unity must be endorsed. This unity must be grasped as something worth fighting and dying for; it must constitute the new foundation for all our political, religious and social reorganization and must provide the theme for our educational systems. Human unity, human understanding, human relationships, human fair play and the essential oneness of all men—these are the only concepts upon which to construct the new world, through which to abolish competition and to bring to an end the exploitation of one section of humanity by another and the hitherto unfair possession of the earth's wealth. As long as there are extremes of riches and poverty men are falling short of their high destiny.

(*Problems of Humanity* 82-3.)

Money, natural resources, energy and its environmental impact, labor, the right use of leisure, and the question of who controls the energy sources are all interrelated factors. They also constitute tremendous problems, none of which have easy solutions. It takes centuries to resolve many of the issues. As far as we can determine, the seventh ray cycling in at this time seems to hold considerable promise for right resolution of these complex problems. Again, the Old Age saw a tendency to separate the spiritual aspirant from mundane worldly affairs. Now the true spiritual aspirant finds great opportunities for service in the worldly institutions of business and economics, politics and governments, science and the environment, as well as in the cultural domain of religion, education, and the arts. The material-form world is seen more and more as an aspect of the spiritual world. As Rudolf Steiner stated: "There is nothing in our world that is not dependent on the spiritual world at every moment. Everything surrounding us is the external expression of the spiritual world. There is no materiality. Everything material is condensed spirit." (*Esoteric Development* 19-20.)

Along with fundamental and far-reaching changes in attitude towards life, death, natural resources, labor, and leisure, there will also be fundamental changes regarding *population*. D.K. suggests a couple of areas where these changes will come.

"The past few hundred years have seen a major problem arise in the present tendency of humanity to collect together in great cities and to congregate in vast herds, leaving the countryside denuded of its population and creating serious problems of sustenance, of health and also of crime. Right before our eyes this rhythm is today changing and a serious problem is being solved; cities are being evacuated and—as men and women are driven forth for one reason or another into the country—the lords of evolution are forcing the breaking up of the rhythm of concentration and substituting for it the rhythm of dispersion. This will do much for the race and will facilitate the unfoldment of a subjective synthesis which will greatly enrich humanity and give new values to living."

(*Externalization of the Hierarchy* 120-1.)

The recent increase in population has to do in part to the success of modern medicine. The negative side of this has to do with the fact that people are often not cured but kept alive beyond the time when they normally would have died. The emphasis has been on the physical mechanism, rather than on the whole of life, which would include the soul. This is one factor that has lead to overpopulation of the planet, with its impact upon economics. "This 'unnatural' preservation of life is the cause of much suffering and is a fruitful source of war, being contrary to the karmic intent of the planetary Logos." (*Esoteric Healing* 278.)

With the incoming of the seventh ray in the 2000 year cycle of the Aquarian Age there will be an increase in sexual activity. This has to do in part with the seventh ray being the major ray that conditions the sacral center in the etheric body. With an increase in the sex drive other problems ensue. According to D.K.:

"The widespread promiscuity of the sexes, and the rule in many countries which entitles a man to possess many wives (which is an insult to the woman), will eventually and inevitably cease. . . . Through this lack of regulation and of essential rhythm, the natural consequences have occurred, and millions of souls have been brought into incarnation who were never intended at this time to incarnate and achieve exoteric manifestation. This fact is largely responsible for much of the present economic distress and for the modern planetary dilemma. The economic situation and the necessity to provide for the unduly large population of the planet lies behind much of the aggression and greed of the nations down the ages, and for the effort being made today as never before to provide better and more adequate living conditions. War has consequently been the inevitable result of this undue and unlimited propagation of the human species. This lack of sexual control has brought into the world thousands of unwanted children whose appearance is solely the result of accidental and uncontrolled sexual relations, and in no way indicates the planned intention of parents— planned because intended to offer experience to incarnating souls, with the conscious intent of offering the opportunity to hasten the "birth into the light" of those particular souls, thus rendering service to the divine plan."

(*Education in the New Age* 135-6.)

Throughout the Alice Bailey books there are a great many insightful observations and ideas that deal with the problem of sex. These passages have been brought together in a book entitled *A Compilation on Sex* published by the Lucis Publishing Co. in New York. Chapter headings include: The Sex Energy, The Problem of Sex, Sex and Discipleship, Marriage and Parenthood, Chakras and Sex Energy, Transmutation and Transference, Kundalini and Sex Energy, Disease and Sex Energy, Homosexuality, The Rays and Sex Energy, Astrology and Sex Energy, Devas and Sex Energy, Cosmic Correspondences to the Sex Impulse, and The Mystery of Sex.

**The Seventh Ray and Healing**. "In many ways," wrote D.K. to one of his students, "you know more about the soul ray which conditions you than you do about your seventh personality ray. Knowledge of this latter ray must come to you through the art of healing, and your soul has rightly led your personality into its right line of activity." (*Discipleship in the New Age*, v. 1, 350.) The rays for this person were as follows:

Soul.................................... II
Personality.......................... 7
    mental body.................. 5
    astral body................... 6
    physical body............... 7

To another student he wrote: "There are two major healing rays among the seven. They are the second and the seventh.... You will note that you are eminently equipped to heal, for you have two streams of second ray energy flowing through you and also two streams of seventh ray energy." (*DNA*, v.1, 641.) The rays in this case were:

Soul.................................... II
Personality.......................... 7
    mental body.................. 4
    astral body................... 2
    physical body............... 7

In a certain sense, disease and sickness are a lack of balance of body chemistry (which depends much on the endocrine system). Sickness also has to do with a lack of balance between the inner psychological bodies and the outer dense physical body. The seventh ray has a great deal to do with homeostasis and the balancing or right relationship of the various forces within the various bodies. When we think of the organization of the seventh ray, we can think of a spiritual-physical organization where everything down to the tiniest detail is in its rightful place. The seventh ray is a ray of synthesis, which implies perfect order, perfect oneness, perfect relationship. Those with the seventh ray in their psychological equipment can work with this "magically" ordering process, which, in a sense, is healing.

The second ray of love-wisdom is apparently also a key ray in the healing process. The second ray is the ray that conditions the heart chakra in the etheric body, which in turn vitalizes the thymus gland. The thymus gland plays a vitally important part in the work of inciting the immunological processes that resist infections and disease. To put it succinctly, love heals.

*With the seventh ray involved in the healing process, what can we speculatively look for in the New Age as this ray becomes more active?* The sixth ray method of healing seems to rely a great deal on faith and devotional prayer. Every religion has its miraculous cures. The fifth ray method of healing (the major ray functioning through modern medicine) deals with extensive knowledge of the form aspect and a manipulation of the form through surgical and chemical means. These two approaches have often been antagonistic to one another. In the extreme cases, some faith healers do not believe in doctors, and some doctors think prayer is nothing but the superstition of the uneducated. It is reasonable to assume that the incoming seventh ray will seek to integrate both of these methods—that is, both science and the spiritual aspects will be intelligently integrated in the healing process. Both the concrete and the relatively abstract—the objective and the subjective—will be recognized as forming parts of one whole and will be utilized in the healing arts-sciences. The psychological causes of disease and imbalance will be investigated. One could say that there will be something like a cross-over in the two fundamental approaches: On the one hand, the spiritual energies and influences will be investigated more scientifically, and on the other, the form will be approached with an appreciation of and an attunement to the spiritual. Already one can see a greater openness to and experimentation with alternative healing methods.

# The Sixth Ray in Transition

In our preceding discussion of the 6th ray and 7th ray, we have emphasized the negative characteristics of the 6th ray. This is not to say that a ray energy, as an expression of divine quality, is negative in the sense of "bad" or "wrong." The negative and reactionary characteristics are strictly human and denote a "crystallized" state—that is, a rigid and tenacious adhering to old established patterns that have outlived their cycle of relative usefulness.

From one perspective, the sixth ray is apparently nearing the completion of its work and can now be used elsewhere in the system. "As the ray influence passes away from a race or a planet, a scheme or a solar system, it must not be supposed that it is completely abrogated; it has simply passed beyond the periphery of whatever ring-pass-not it was energizing, and the force of its influence is being focused elsewhere.   The original recipient becomes a channel, or a transmitting agent, and not so much an absorber or container....   When the cycle is drawing to a close, more and more of the ray influence or magnetism will be felt elsewhere, until practically all of it will be passed on unabsorbed." (*Treatise on Cosmic* Fire 439.)

*What is the work that the sixth ray has accomplished relative to human development?*  What has been the positive labor of the sixth ray over the past 2000 years?   In many respects this ray is still very much with us.  We are told that there are still a large number of sixth ray souls in incarnation at this time, "for it will be about  two hundred years before all the sixth ray egos pass out of incarnation." (*Eso. Psych.*, v.1,26.)  In order to obtain a whole and balanced picture of the sixth ray—and in order not to fall into the negative side of the sixth ray itself by presenting a one-sided pic- ture of the sixth ray—let us consider some of the significant accomplishments of this ray energy during the past two millennia.

**Good Taste**.  "The instinct which has characterized this passing sixth  ray period  and which has been noticeably fostered under its influence is that of *taste*—taste in food, in human intercourse, in color, in form, in art and architecture, and in all branches of human knowledge. This discriminating taste has reached a relatively high stage of development during the past two thousand years and 'good taste' is a highly cherished mass virtue and objective today. This is a totally new thing and one which has been hitherto the prerogative of the highly cultured few. (*Destiny of Nations* 114.)

Taste has to do with a feeling for beauty and a feeling for quality, and, as such, there is a relationship here with taste and the 6th ray, with the higher astral plane, with a feeling for the ideal, and with the 4th ray of harmony and beauty. On a higher level the sense of good taste becomes a "discriminating sense of values."

To help one appreciate this point about taste, it might be helpful for the reader to reflect for a moment on those who do not have a developed sense of good taste. The opposite of good taste could be seen as a kind of crudeness and lack of discrimination. Crudeness is often indicative of a preponderance of lower astral energy. In the very long line of development between animal-man and god-man, lower astral energy is more indicative of the early animal-man stages. It is interesting to think of the Piscean Age and the 6th ray as having to do with the work of *elevating the masses* from degrees of crudeness to levels of aristocratic taste.

**Non-Materialistic.** "Under the immediate expression of the sixth ray, the divine principle of desire has shifted potently away from the desire for material form into the realm of higher desire. Though materialism is still rampant, there are few people who are not animated by certain definite idealistic aspirations for which they are ready, when needed, to make sacrifices. This is a relatively new phenomenon and one that should be carefully noted." (*Destiny* 133.)

One of the difficulties or negative factors of the incoming 7th ray—as it conditions the physical-etheric plane—is that in some cases it could augment materialistic attitudes. The form of things, disconnected from soul and spirit, could loom too large in the minds of men. The great value of the 6th ray can be seen as a predecessor of the 7th ray. The 6th ray prepared the ground by

101

cultivating spiritual aspiration and the connection to spirit. One might use the analogy of the lifetime of an individual. During the stage of youth, there should be plenty of 6th ray aspiration and idealism. The youthful ones are natural visionaries; they tend to see things not as they are but as they should be and could be. If there isn't sufficient 6th ray idealism present in youth, then the mature person will probably be a materialist, working almost exclusively for self and form.

**Capacity for Abstraction.**

The second objective of the sixth ray disciple or of the man who is emerging out of the sixth ray influence but is still conditioned by it (being a representative human being from the current evolutionary angle) has been the unfolding of the "capacity for abstraction," as it has been called. The outstanding quality of our day and period, as a result of transmuting human quality and character in and through its disciples, has been the expression of the idealistic nature of man, or of his instinctual response to the higher intuitional values. In the past, highly developed but rare people have here and there demonstrated this power to abstract the consciousness from the material or form side of life and to focus it upon the ideal and upon the formless expression of living truth. Today, whole masses of people and entire nations are regimented to certain forms of idealism and can and do appreciate ideas, formulated into ideals. Thus again the success of the evolutionary process can be seen and the work of the Hierarchy, as it endeavors to expand human consciousness, can be demonstrated to be effective.

*Destiny of Nations* 113.

This is very similar to the earlier points mentioned above, but it is presented from a slightly different angle, which serves to help us understand some of the subtleties of the ray energies. When one chooses one religion over another, or when one votes for one political candidate instead of another, one is really attuning to an ideal and to an abstract idea. During the Middle Ages, the king selected the religion for the nation. During the Middle Ages, there was very little democracy. The common person had not yet reached the point where he or she could reflect adequately upon the abstract concepts presented by various religions and various political interests. Peasants at that time were considered childlike in their devotion to or response to the authority of dukes and kings. Democracy was unthinkable at the time. Nowadays, and evidently as a result of the long work of the 6th ray energy, more and more people can "appreciate ideas, formulated into ideals." In order to navigate in the sea of ideals, ideas, and abstractions, refined astral sensitivities are required. Usually we tend to think of the capacity to make discriminative choices, simply as a capacity of mind, of intelligence. But on closer examination we see that refined feelings plays an equally important role..

**The Principle of Recognition and Evoking Desire for the Materializing of an Ideal..** Here, once again, we are looking at much the same thing, but from a slightly different angle.

The sixth Ray of Devotion embodies the principle of recognition. By this I mean the capacity to see the ideal reality lying behind the form; this implies a one-pointed application of desire and of intelligence in order to produce an expression of that sensed idea. It is responsible for much of the formulation of the ideas which have led man on, and for much of the emphasis on the appearance which has veiled and hidden those ideals. It is on this ray primarily—as it cycles in and out of manifestation—that the work of distinguishing between appearance and quality is carried forward, and this work has its field of activity upon the astral plane. The complexity of this subject and the acuteness of the feeling evolved become therefore apparent.

*Esoteric Psychology*, vol. 1, 52.

D.K. mentions in *Esoteric Psychology* that 6th ray people need handling with care due to the fact that they are sensitive and full of personal desire. He also mentions that their method of "evoking desire for the materializing of an ideal is indispensable, and, fortunately, there are many aspirants and disciples on this ray available today." (EP, v.2,144.)

This type of person has the ability to inspire others to do the necessary work. When they speak, they can touch feelings that link with soul, and thus transcend lower intellectual mind. They are not intellectually dry and pedantic. They are not manipulative and clever. They bring in a special zeal and a special passion to the work. They kindle fiery aspiration in others.

D.K. makes the following statement in *Rays and Initiation*: "To many what I will say will be as meaningless as *A Treatise on Cosmic Fire* is to the average reader and as the entire theme of initiation is to the ignorant and the undeveloped man. Much, however, should be of practical service to the struggling disciple, and I want in these concluding pages to fire his zeal, deepen his understanding, stimulate his capacity to love, and enlighten his mind. Such is what I seek to do." (RI 329.) Kindling the aspiration, firing the zeal, or evoking desire in the right way is an *indispensable* part of the work of bringing in the new ideas through the materializing of the right ideals.

Perhaps the need for this is most easily seen in the field of education. As D.K. mentioned in *Education in the New Age*, young people need "to feel and rightly feel beauty, strength and wisdom." The great art and skill of the teacher has to do with being able to bring the ideas appropriately unto the plane of feeling in order to kindle aspiration in the young. When dry, intellectual concepts are given to the children and they are asked to memorize them, there results an education that is essentially without soul. So here again one can think deeply about the value of the 6th ray energy of idealism, and one can bring appreciation for its right manifestation.

# SOME QUESTIONS ANSWERED

**Soul and Personality Rays**. Question: *"Why are the rays of the soul and the personalities of the disciples given in the books never the same? I mean, could a person have a seventh ray soul and a seventh ray personality? Is this a rule or isn't it?"*

This is a good, fundamental, and important question. The principles involved here are BALANCE and WHOLENESS. The ray of the soul stays the same for a long time and through many incarnations (although in some cases it does change). The ray of the personality, however, changes from one incarnation to the next. In a certain sense, the personality ray is like a sub-ray of the soul ray. A 1st ray soul would not work through a 1st ray personality for some long time. That would be too destructive, too powerful. The impact on others would be too devastating. The person would end up destroying himself. A 1st ray soul could have a 1st ray personality, but that would only happen (it seems to me and from what I have studied) after the soul has been seasoned, or fully developed, or rounded-out, and whole. The 1st ray soul would have to have something of all the other rays in it, so that it is whole and balanced.

**Color and the Rays**. Question: *"Do the seven rays correspond to the seven colors of the light spectrum that comprise our visible universe?"*

This is one of those questions that would have to be answered: Yes and no. *Color, sound, and number* are, esoterically speaking, very profound matters—too profound for us to venture any kind of comprehensive definition here.. D.K. goes into this matter at some length in the book: *Letters on Occult Meditation*. We quote a few passages below:

"Colors as manifested on the physical plane show at their crudest and harshest. Even the most exquisite of shades as seen by the physical eye is hard and harsh compared to those on the emotional plane, and as the finer matter of the other planes is contacted, the beauty, the softness and the exquisite quality of the different hues grow with each transition. When the ultimate and synthetic color is reached the beauty transcends all conception."

"The very use of the word 'Color' shows the intention, for, as you know, the definition of the word conveys the idea of concealment. Color is therefore 'that which does conceal.' It is simply the objective medium by means of which the inner force transmits itself; it is the reflection upon matter of the type of influence that is emanating from the Logos, and which has penetrated to the densest part of His solar system. We recognize it as *color*. The adept knows it as differentiated force, and the initiate of the higher degree knows it as *ultimate light*, undifferentiated and undivided."

"Color is but the form assumed by force, of some kind, when that force is moving at a certain measure, and when its action and movement is impeded or unimpeded by the material through which it plays. In this sentence lies the key to the solution of the problem as to the color differences on the higher planes and on the lower. The resistance of matter to the downflow of force or life, and its relative density or rarity accounts for much of the color distinction." *Letters on Occult Meditation*, pp. 209, 210-11, 232.)

**The Rays of Brazil**. Question: *I wonder if you have some study of Brazil's rays, and its role in the world of nations? I know that the part that Brazil is going to play lies far ahead in the future, and that, according to D.K., Brazil is a probationary disciple. Nevertheless the Hierarchy works for the future, and the future's harvest must be seeded or sowed at the present.*

We do not have a study on the rays of Brazil. Some of our students have a keen interest in the rays of their nation. To me this is a most fascinating study. Wherever possible, I try to encourage others to pursue this interest-study, and I try to work along with them in some capacity. In the future (not the distant future)

106

perhaps we could bring out a book that would include several people and their thoughts about the rays of their nation and also their thoughts about other nations as well. This could prove helpful to many others. Also it could prove helpful in bringing about something like a global consciousness along spiritual lines. We hear much about the global economy, but it would be helpful if we heard more about the psychological connections and brotherhood between nations.

As you mention, D.K. states that "Brazil is on the Path of Probation and will rapidly move forward" (*Esoteric Psychology*, p. 265). Isn't that wonderful. I imagine that already since the time of that writing Brazil has made significant strides forward. Brazil's music, of course, is what we hear about first here in the US, and this relates to its 4th ray contribution.

"The future harvest must be seeded or sowed at the present." Yes. yes! And it is a great joy to be involved in some way in sowing those seeds. The motto of Brazil, as you undoubtedly know, is "I hide the seed." The little seed and the little new plant (the seedling) is delicate. It holds within it the great promise and glory of the future. The plan and program is already contained in the little seed. Those workers who work with the nurturing of the seeds are like the mother who wipes away each tear and feeds the young one with love, seeing the future in the right attention given to each little baby step forward. This also ties in closely with the theme of Virgo (that important sign of nurturing, which requires getting the details right in the delicate early stages), which is the sign of Brazil's personality. Brazil and the United States are linked via the 2nd ray of love wisdom (U.S. soul ray and Brazil's personality ray), and also via Mercury (the Virgo-Gemini connection, for the U.S., has a Gemini personality).

Brazil has to do with nothing less than the birth of the future 6th root race. The present 5th root race brings forth the development of mind and intellect. The 6th race will add to this the development of intuition, which will then once again link humanity to divinity, and place humankind back within the divine circulatory flow. We can see the importance of the 4th ray of harmony through conflict in this process, for it is the ray of the 4th

107

plane of buddhi (intuition). As you know, the 4th ray is not in incarnation at this time (few 4th ray souls) but is destined to return around 2025, and already preliminary work goes forward. The two rays that will condition and dominate the intuitive 6th race are the 2nd ray and the 4th ray, which , as you know, are the rays of Brazil.

Your own thoughts on the rays of your nation, your thoughts on the state of affairs presently in Brazil, and your thoughts on the play of esotericism and the intuition in Brazil would be a much interest to us. We would like to share some of your thoughts in our newsletter from time to time, for others would surely benefit from them.

**Rays of the Mind.** Question: *The observation and radionic analysis of my patients, acquaintances and the members of my family yield the following results, in terms of the mental ray. I have analyzed 43 people:*

*1st ray mind........14%*
*2nd ray mind........0*
*3rd ray mind.........0*
*4th ray mind.........9.5%*
*5th ray mind.........46%*
*6th ray mind.........21 %*
*7th ray mind.........9.5%*

*In the study work you have mentioned that the mind may be on the 1st, the 4th, and the 5th rays. In other literature you can find other rays for the mind. Why do you specify only certain rays for the mind?*

That is a very good question. It is necessary to be very clear on this matter.

D.K. sorts out some of the complexities of the seven rays by giving us the following facts:

Soul....................on any one of the 7 rays.
Personality...........on any one of the seven rays.
mental body..............ray 1, 4, or 5.....on 5th plane.
emotional body.........ray 2 or 6...........on 6th plane.
physical body............ray 3 or 7...........on 7th plane.

It stands to reason that the *body would be conditioned by the ray of that plane*, generally speaking. The lower triplicity is then 5-6-7. The lower triangle has a *higher correspondence*, the higher being: 1-2-3. Devotion (6) becomes love (2). Physical rhythm (7) becomes active intelligence (3). And mental development, the ability to think (5) becomes power (1). The 4th ray is the mediator, the messenger, between the lower and the higher. The human kingdom is the fourth kingdom and is intimately involved in the work of transmuting the lower into the higher. We gain consciousness through the rays of attribute and can eventually function within the rays of aspect.

In the unfoldment and creation of things there are exceptions to the rule—there always are. The above general rule was given out in three of D.K.'s books: *Esoteric Psychology*, v.1, p.320-1; *Esoteric Psychology*, v.2, p. 288; *Glamour: A World Problem*, p.92. He tells us that the information is "of profound psychological interest and import," (EP,v.1). In the 2nd vol. he states: "The above tabulation is one of the most important ever made in this Treatise in connection with psychology." In *Glamour* he states: "This statement as to the governing rays is a statement of an *infallible rule*, except in the case of accepted disciples."

In the book *Discipleship in the New Age*, D.K. gives the rays of those whom he instructed. There were:

| Ray of Mind | Number of Persons | percentage |
|---|---|---|
| **1st ray** | 6 | **16%** |
| 2nd | 3 | 8% |
| 3rd | 2 | 5% |
| **4th** | **19** | **51%** |
| **5th** | **7** | **19%** |
| 6th | 0 | 0 |
| 7th | 0 | 0 |
| total | 37 | |

In the case of these 37 developed people, 86% follow the 1st, 4th, or 5th ray general rule.

D.K. mentions in *Rays and Initiations* (p.570, 574) that a 7th ray mind occurs at a certain stage of evolutionary development. He also mentions that the Buddha had a 6th ray mind "a very rare phenomena," *Destiny of Nations*, p.38. *Thus, it is true that the mind can be on any one of the 7 rays.* The general rule, however, is 1,4, and 5. The exception to the rule can occur in the more developed person.

It seems to me that the least desirable mental ray would be the 6th ray. This would tend to make the mind have an "idee fixe", as it used to be called, or to have a tendency to have something like obsessions. It seems to me that the Buddha, in order to make a tremendous break through to the balanced Middle Path and a new level of enlightenment, was given the *handicap* of a 6th ray mind. The 6th ray mind did not help him find the Middle Path, for it made him at first (before his enlightenment) an extremist or a fanatic. Initially, he was extremely devotional to whatever path he found. He carried all the extreme methods to the last degree, so that he and others would be clear as to their final outcome. He then gave up all paths and sat under the bodi tree, vowing not to move until he *knew*, or until enlightenment came. This, in itself, and somewhat ironically, had some 6th ray quality in it. The break through led to a new type of spiritual path and a new level of enlightenment for humanity. Right action, for example, is not the extreme of no action, or the extreme of excessive action. Both of those methods lead to an imbalance. The Middle Path is *Right Action*. Profoundly simple, yet not readily understood, and definitely not easy.

It could be said that as a spiritual duty or task (dharma), the Buddha was given not a path of least resistance, but a path of the greatest resistance. He had to know, presumably, that all the popular paths of the day were *not* the way to the higher enlightenment (or the next higher level of consciousness to which humanity was given access), and he had to know this beyond any shadow of a doubt. Perhaps we could say that Buddhism is the least fanatical of the well-known world religions. Through the stupendous effort of that great World Teacher, the balanced Middle Path was brought to the Piscean Age and still brings much benefit to humankind.

You are quite right, however, in saying that the mind can be on any one of the seven rays. Consider the above material simply as background for your own experiments and for your own efforts to determine the rays and to work with the rays. It is a new and important field of endeavor. We must keep an open mind and explore many avenues as we patiently gather knowledge and experience in the fascinating field.

**The Pentagram.** Question: *"My point of view is that the Pentagram includes 3-fold personality, the soul, and the New Group of World Servers. What I would like to know is if I am right about this."*

The Pentagram is a very profound symbol with many meanings and many levels of meaning. Looking at it from one level, it has to do with Perfected Man - Fivefold Man. This would be God-Man or Initiate. This is a major goal of evolution. This would include physical-emotional-mental man (as you rightly say, the threefold personality), plus soul, plus buddhi or the 4th plane of intuition. You have then:

1........buddhi, intuition
2........soul, higher mind
3........mental body, lower mind, intellect
4........emotional body
5........physical body

We have then FIVE. The implications of this is enormous. The Middle Principle here is the mental body. I ask you: which way will it turn? There is the lower three, and the higher three - with the mind participating in either triangle. Which way will it turn? The mind is the middle principle here, a sort of pivotal point. The drama unfolds on the mental plane (the FIFTH plane). The Fifth Ray plays a major role. The drama is connected to the Life of Venus - a Fifth Ray Planet - a planet that stands to our Earth as the Soul to Personality. The Earth is a Third Ray Planet. The implications are enormous - we need not contemplate all of them.

Five has to do with the Fifth Race. Which way will it choose? The way of order-control and scientific materialism - and thus lose connection with soul and negate spirit? Or will it discover the way of the Heart and subordinate form to spirit, so that spirit and form can work with perfected unity in Perfected Man or God-Man?

111

**The Even Armed Cross**. Question-Statement: *Regarding your "basic esoteric meanings of the equal-armed cross," I would agree with you that it "seems reasonable to place the seal of quality at the intersection. Its attractiveness tends to unite the higher and lower vertical, while its radiation 'fills' the horizontal."*

I think of the even-armed cross as *a cross*, that is, a square, which suggests conflict, pain, friction, and opposites, as opposed to *the triangle*, which suggests integration, unity, a cooperation, and a blending of energies. The Sagittarian reaches very high into Cosmos—higher than any other sign. Indeed, this ability to reach into intuitive realms is one of its great gifts to other signs. Jupiter plays a role in this intuitive expansiveness, as does *the vertical arm of the cross*. Esoterically, Sagittarius is brought down to the non-sacred planet of Earth. The spiritual-philosophical insights must somehow be applied in service to others. No easy task. The aspirant becomes the serving disciple. He then lives with a certain amount of pain (of the cross) knowing that it is inescapable, but sensing also something of the secret joy that he works for others and for the future. In this self-sacrificing and sacrificial work, *radiance* becomes subtly evident. The radiance draws others on and up. The "quality at the intersection" we could probably term soul or Christ. This Crucified Christ works with those who are at the stage of the Hidden Christ. The "stage" following the *service through crucifixion* is the Living Risen Christ. There is great strength and power in this radiance that knows no death. One cannot kill Spirit, let alone touch it. "Its radiation *'fills'* the horizontal," as you say. This radiance is what is attractive. What links the higher and the lower, however, may be more *intent, motive, will, and purpose*.

**Rays of the United States**. Question: You mention that the *"national political campaigns and associated rhetoric is somewhat related to the ray energies of the United States"* [The U.S. has a 2nd ray soul and a 6th ray personality]," and you speculate as to the possibility of the 2nd ray being subordinate to the 6th ray, or *"Have the 2nd ray tendencies been co-opted by the sixth ray so that the latter is really primary while the former,* *appearing substantial, is really a 'sub-ray' of the sixth ray and controlled by it?"*

Interesting question. As we study the rays, we begin to have little insights as to how they play out through people and through groups and nations. It is always interesting to consider what political leaders touch the soul of the nation, and which ones appeal primarily to the personality energy. The subtlety of your analysis brings the further question of whether or not a candidate is able to appear 2nd ray, when in fact the 6th ray quality dominates? Personally I think you are quite correct in your observation. I think that some candidates are able to identify the popularity of certain second ray qualities (such as the warm smile, the sense of unity, the heart going out to the less fortunate, etc.) and are able to present the qualities or talk about the qualities, without really living them in any substantial way.

**Psychiatrists and the Spiritual Dimension**. Statement: *"It is imperative that psychiatrists include some understanding of the spiritual dimension in people's lives."* Also, the religious question is very important, for it can *"hold the potential for tremendous healing, growth, and inner-transformation."*

Yes, yes! In my view that is an extremely important observation. I have counseled for the last six years people who have been under the care of the mental health professionals. This matter has come up again and again. I feel this point you are making perhaps as deeply as you do.

People like Carl Jung certainly understood much of the "spiritual dimension in people's lives."

The religious problem or question seems to be something that many of the professionals either avoid, ignore, or, as you indicate, consider symptomatic. That has troubled me, because, if one listens very closely for some length of time, one can often see that there are several seeds of potential healing hidden within the religious confusion and discussion. Also, the meaning and the symbolism of what the clients are trying to express go far beyond the limitations of the rational mind and go far beyond the narrowness of simply conforming to basic material functions. In other words, they are struggling for their mental well-being in a

113

rather crazy world. Their religious struggles and questions will very often carry them in the right direction. We should not negate them, for they are often part of the solution.

It is true, however, that the religious focus may appear to be part of the problem also. One technique that seems to work for me is the following: When a person appears to be deeply troubled and when the person is discussing at some length the Bible and other religious matters, invariably the energy is predominantly and strongly a 6th ray energy. The emotions are usually strong, the mental development varies. Initially, I work *with* the 6th ray energy. This means listening at length with understanding and recognizing the truth of what they are saying. One has to really see the truth of it and not just agree in a superficial way. One must avoid the tendency to show them that the opposite of what they say may also be true. I try to stay with them in their truth for some time. As I express understanding, they relax. Through understanding I gradually fill the relation-discussion with second ray energy, which has to do with love and appreciation for them and their struggle. In the right way and at the right time, one can bring the discussion to Christ and Christ's love. They sense, or truly know, that this *is the way*, and it is a way that we can truly call salvation. Christ and His words are not brought in as a point of rational argument, however. They are brought in more as a gentle question: How would Christ handle this, or what would Christ say? or something like that.

Their 6th ray expression—which is one-pointed and not devoid of fanaticism—has certain seeds of destruction in it as well as pointing the way towards healing. The 6th ray attitude can get very fearful, or worried, or hateful towards others. If they go round and round with the negative attitude, their mental state will not be good. When one sees the truth of it, they do relax the attitude, and then, using their own words and their own book, the healing quality of love and patience and understanding can come into play. One's own aura becomes a healing catalysis for them. Once the love begins to settle the solar plexus center, then it is always good to inject humor. Humor and laughter are also great healers, as many know. And then new activity (which emerges from *within them*) helps to get them to move forward, since positive activity is also very healing.

**The Role of Desire.** Question: *Is desire in its great many forms, both in terms of grasping and rejecting—desire for affection, love, security through money, power, etc.; desire for beauty and harmony and so on—is desire not a result of the 2nd ray energy of our solar system?*

As I try to enter into the feeling and meaning of your words, I appreciate this sense of *desire* being a very large, pervasive, all-encompassing phenomenon that reaches to Deity Itself—something behind the evolutionary process.

If it does go from the molecule to Deity, there are still great and fundamental differences from one level to another (as well as similarities). We could think of it as functioning on various levels:

Intuition.................spiritual desire...the will of God
                    made known.

Soul, higher mind....desire for the good of the whole.

Intellect..................intellectual desire, ideas-plans of
                    personal benefit.

Emotion..................personal likes-dislikes.

Physical..................instinctual desire, automatic
                    attraction-repulsion.

If we look at it in terms of *level* then right away we can see that it manifests in a very different way from one level to the next. We could also think of it in terms of the levels of the different chakras.

Head.....................will of God, the desire to blend the
                    little will with the Will of God.

Ajna.....................personal will, choice between two
                    ways—the two paths.

Heart....................good of the group, good of the whole,
                    self-sacrifice.

Throat..................intellect, ideas, the will (desire) to
                    know.

Solar plexus..........desire for a full emotional life—
                    excitement, adventure.

Sacral center.........desire for sexual completeness.

Base of spine........the most fundamental desire, the
                    desire to live, the will-to-live.

If we think of it in terms of the life of the soul and the life of the personality, then we have something like this:

SOUL
Sacrificial Will

Love (higher feeling)     Light (knowledge)

PERSONALITY
intellect          sentience

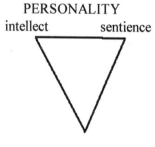

physical nature

One could say that the downward looking triangle of personality is filled with personal desire (which can be detrimental to the good of the whole). The upward looking triangle is filled with the desire for the group good, which implies personal sacrifice.

Why does God create something that has a personal desire that can be detrimental to the good of the whole? One could say that animal *instinct* follows the code of Deity. It is not out of the Divine Circulatory Flow. The Gods, of course, Those in the Higher Kingdoms, the Kingdom of Heaven, are within the Divine Flow (although there are sacred and non-sacred planets). It is the Human Family—part animal and part god—that is sometimes within the Flow and sometimes very disruptively out of the Divine Flow.

Yet God created this situation. The question is why? Perhaps we could say it is created for purposes of developing *consciousness*. You mention the factor of the 2nd Solar System, and you mention in this regard the 2nd ray. As you know, the 1st Solar System dealt with the Form (and the 3rd ray), the 2nd present Solar System develops Consciousness (the 2nd ray), and the 3rd Solar System (along with the 1st ray) develops Will.

When the energy comes through a person in an instinctual way, then the responses are predictable and automatic. But there is very little consciousness.

If we desire something, *we want it*, and we take action to get it. This suggests that desire is perhaps more a *factor of will* than it is of the 2nd ray of love.

The intellectual mind along with emotion-feeling develops the in-between body of kama-manas, which has been translated desire-mind. Here we have desire linked to the 2nd aspect of personality, the emotional aspect, with its bundle of likes-and-dislikes.

And, of course, desire, as mentioned, on the physical level is automatic instinctual desire, which is connected to the activity of the 3rd ray and the building of the Form aspect, as in the 1st Solar System.

The "desire" of soul is not personal. Its main quality and intent is to be of *service to others*, so the energy is one of *giving*. The desire of personality is *to get*, which is all right at first, as the personality grows through experiment and experience.

"There is no desire left for the separated self. Kama-manas disappears, and man is then regarded as consisting essentially of soul-mind-brain, within the body nature. This is a great mystery, and its significance can only be understood when a man has controlled his personality and eliminated all aspects of glamour and of illusion. This is accomplished by accomplishing. This mastery is achieved by mastering. This elimination of desire is brought about by conscious eliminating." *Glamour*, p. 66. Here the word desire designates the kama-manas energy.

"Under the immediate expression of the sixth ray, the divine principle of desire has shifted potently away from the desire for material form into the realm of higher desire." (*Destiny of Nations*,

117

113.) Desire here is still on the emotional plane, but it is the higher levels of that plane, bringing aspiration for something higher.

"Service is a life demonstration. It is a soul urge, and is as much an evolutionary impetus of the soul as the urge to self-preservation or to the reproduction of the species is a demonstration of the animal soul. This is a statement of importance. It is a soul instinct, if we may use such an inadequate expression and is, therefore, innate and peculiar to soul unfoldment. It is the outstanding characteristic of the soul, just as desire is the outstanding characteristic of the lower nature. It is group desire, just as in the lower nature it is personality desire." *Esoteric Psychology*, v.1,125. Here we find a higher correspondence, the "group desire" of the soul.

"It is not difficult to manifest creativeness of spirit when thought seeks to picture the Universe as an unconfined domain. In the desire to alter its conception, humanity already moves forward. Manifest the desire for new images. Manifest the desire for new paths. Having awakened the desire toward the beauty of Infinity in everything, humanity will walk forward without glancing back. Only the grandeur of Cosmos will impel the spirit toward the Inaccessible Heights." *Infinity I*, paragraph 46.

"To desire means to find the gates of the Subtle World. But it is difficult for people to learn to desire. They cannot bring their feelings into equilibrium and so they cannot create unwavering, unconquerable desire. Verily, desire is a creative lever in the Subtle World. This power came from the Highest World, but it also demands the clarity of the Highest World. When we direct you along the line of Hierarchy, We prepare you for this sovereignty, the clarity of desire. Amidst the intercrossing of currents of the lowest sphere it is not so easy to detect the purified desire that is like an arrow. One can conquer the pressure of the earthly atmosphere by striving to the highest; therefore Hierarchy is the sole outlet." *Heart*, paragraph 198. In these last two quotes from Master M. we see something of the will touching the human being on the level of the higher aspiring feeling nature.

118

**New Group of World Servers**. Question: *Can you explain to me the meaning of the phrase: "The greater Ashram, composed of many Ashrams, is the fulfilled production of the New Group of World Servers, down the ages."* (Discipleship in the New Age, *v.2, 201.) Does this mean that the New Group of World Servers (NGWS) (which was proclaimed only recently) produced the Hierarchy personnel down the ages? Or does this mean that it will be so in the Aquarian Age? What can you say about this?*

I would say that the first of your two speculations is the correct one. The NGWS down the ages produced the Hierarchical personnel. Or phrasing it from the other perspective: The Hierarchy has gathered its personnel out of the NGWS down the ages. (This may not be the only source for Hierarchical personnel, particularly in the early stages of its formation.) The confusion here is the contradiction: If there has been a NGWS down the ages, then why is it called the *New Group* of World Servers? I would think that what DK is referring to is an Intermediate Group between Hierarchy and Humanity that plays greater and lesser roles during different times. There are always intermediate "bodies" being developed between two major bodies. For example, (using the Law of Analogy) there is the astral body and the mental body. When these two work "together" during a certain stage of development, then the intermediate *kama-manasic body* is developed. The kama-manasic body is particularly strong during a certain stage of evolution. When the mind or manasic body becomes strongly developed, then the kama-manasic body recedes and eventually disappears.

There is something *new* about the NGWS and there is something about it that has been with us a long time. The NGWS, as an intermediary body between Hierarchy and Humanity, has been with us a long time, but technically one might call it something else when referring to years long past. One might call it the Group of Intermediary Servers. What makes it *new* now is the fact that we have *world* servers. Therefore, there is something *new* about this intermediary body. It is a bigger group, and it is global in consciousness. And it is receiving a lot of attention from Hierarchy as a group. Never before have there been so many people participating in this group, and never before have the personnel of this group been gathered from *all over the world*. And never before has this group had such a world influence.

**The Problem of Intellect and the Need for Soul in Education**.

An important question comes up again and again in the work of developing an education that is inclusive of the spiritual dimensions, and that question is: How to define "soul"? Of course, there must be clear definition. One must be very careful here, however, so that one avoids the lower concrete mind's tendency to "slay the real." Anything overly intellectualized tends to lose its deeper meaning. Words themselves change their connotation as personality and intellect fail to rise to true significance and original meaning. In the Alice Bailey books there are many clear and illuminating definitions of soul, several of which are in the compilation *The Soul, the Quality of Life*.

Often, one of the better ways to comprehend soul is to see it not as a duality - a higher vague spiritual something hovering above a more visible personality - but to see it within a triplicity - a middle sphere in the basic, all-pervading, and relative triplicity. This then tends to reveal the true whole within which the soul is a vital part.

The basic triplicity of personality is thinking-feeling-doing, or mental body, emotional body, physical-etheric body. This triplicity within the grasp of everyone provides an analogy which enables access to the greater triplicities, listed below.

spirit......... consciousness....matter-form
life............. quality.............. appearance
monad........ soul................. personality
purpose.......love-wisdom....active intelligence
atma.......... buddhi............. manas
will............ intuition.......... mind
head........... heart.............. throat.

The world of form-appearance is easy to "prove" due to its visibility and density. Many of the more materialistic thinkers have a difficult time accepting such relative abstractions as "emotional love" or a sum-total of characteristics commonly recognized as "personality," not to mention the even finer vibratory rate of group

120

consciousness, intuition, and the light, love, and purpose of the threefold soul.

The soul is the second aspect and has to do with such very real things as love, wisdom, quality, intuition, awareness, illumination, the good of the whole, and heart. The present emphasis in education is on the form or third aspect. This has to do with the development of intellect, with identifying the intricacies of the form world, and with preparing one vocationally for participation in a rather materialistically focused society.

Is there anything particularly wrong with this? According to Rudolph Steiner: "If man were not to develop anything else but intelligence, he would become an evil being on earth. If we want to think of a wholesome future for mankind, we must not count on the one-sided development of intelligence." He said that it is becoming "more and more impossible to recognize the good through mere intelligence" (Education as a Social Problem, p.85). One could say that a soulless education in a materialistic world is a slow death.

The Tibetan teacher, D.K. writes: "I would here remind you that it is the expansion of consciousness and the production of increased sensitivity and perceptive awareness which is the goal of all divine and hierarchical effort. The goal is not for betterment of material conditions. These will automatically follow when the sense of awareness is steadily unfolded. The future of humanity is determined by its aspiration and ability to respond to the idealism which is today flooding the world." (*Education in the New Age*, 103.)

The Master Morya writes: "You are right in desiring to give school children an understanding of the whole boundlessness of creative activity. Why endure with new radiance the garment of a grandfather? Try to resemble builders of new powerful bridges, and strive toward the radiance of the higher worlds. Not phantasmagoria of life!" (*Infinity*, v.1, pp.35-36). He also writes: "The child's heart recognizes what is aflame and what is extinguished. Not the given lesson but the mutual aspiration of teacher and pupil reveals the world of wonders. To open the eyes of a pupil means to share with him the love of great creation." (*Fiery World*, v.1, p.320.)

Rudolph Steiner said that the most important qualities a teacher brings to the classroom are enthusiasm and interest. "Intellectual life has very little to do with the true interests of human beings! I ask you: how many teachers do you not see today, passing in and out of higher and lower educational institutions without bringing any inner enthusiasm to their science but pursuing it merely as a means of livelihood? In such cases the interest of the soul is not directly linked with the actual pursuit. The same thing happens even at school. Think how much is learned at the various stages of life without any real enthusiasm or interest, how external the intellectual life is becoming for many people who devote themselves to it! And how many there are today who are forced to produce a mass of intellectual material which is then preserved in libraries and, as spiritual life, is not really alive!" (*The Influences of Lucifer and Ahriman*, p.47).

If we reflect deeply on these qualities of enthusiasm and interest, we will see that they are sparked by the fire of spirit and they result in greater soul consciousness. Enthusiasm, in this sense, with its "new" energy burns through the lethargy of boredom and the inertia of personal comfort. With enthusiasm and interest we also find a blending of something of the will (the driving energy of enthusiasm) and of love (the more passive yet expanding energy of interest), yielding eventually an illuminated intelligence - a mind that reveals the real instead of slaying the real.

Extrapolating from the above, one could say that as soul educators, in no matter what school or setting, there are certain questions that one tends to ask oneself on an almost daily basis:
• Can I find what is especially interesting about the subject matter and present it with fascination and enthusiasm?
• The soul lends its magical touch in different ways at different developmental stages. Do I see how the soul touches the particular age-stage of my students or am I projecting my own level-stage onto them?
• Kindled interest leads to expansion of consciousness, which then leads to new activities. Interest never hovers only in the abstract. As an educator am I able to spark interest and provide creative release in new activities?

• Do I care deeply enough for the children or young people with whom life has brought me in contact? Am I able to detach from any personal likes and dislikes so that I can begin to see into the person's soul?

• What are the hidden qualities in each child, tentatively seeking expression? Can I help the child bring out his/her spiritual qualities, as well as personality skills, and help her/him circulate them in the pool of the group life?

• The seven keywords for soul education are: Interest, Enthusiasm, Inspiration, Expansion, Love, Patience, Understanding. Am I careful not to harm, through excessive form insistence, but to nurture the delicate budding interests as they emerge from fresh soul?

• Do I treat the young people as soul equals? Can I relate soul to soul? Am I deepening my friendship with each child on a daily basis?

• Am I over-emphasizing the form of the curriculum? Or am I ensouling the curriculum in such a way that learning becomes a joy?

• Do I see the relativity of form and the continuity of Soul?

• Am I the dramatic one at the center? Or can I let the center shift from me to them? Can I stand in a peripheral manner to the center of their learning?

• Are we teaching from and to the immeasurable, unquantifiable soul?

• M.M. writes: "Feeling will always prevail over reason.... Reason cannot create if the seed of the heart is not provided" (*Heart*, paragraph. 391). Am I teaching in such a way that pupils "feel and rightly feel Beauty, Strength, and Wisdom," and Justice, Purpose, and Truth?

# BOOKS and SCHOOLS
## for FURTHER STUDY

**The Alice Bailey Books and the Arcane School.** The great teaching on the Seven Rays has been given forth in the Alice Bailey books. The books of special importance on this subject are the five volume series known as the *Treatise on the Seven Rays.* The five volumes are:

Vol. I—Esoteric Psychology
Vol. II—Esoteric Psychology
Vol. III—Esoteric Astrology
Vol. IV—Esoteric Healing
Vol. V— Rays and Initiations.

Other Bailey books that deal with additional seven ray related subject matter include the following: *The Destiny of Nations* discusses the rays of nations. *Discipleship in the New Age*, vol. I and II, includes a series of letter written to several of D.K.'s disciples or students. This letters go into specific detail in regard to a person's psychological ray make-up. These are the main monumental books that focus on the far-reaching and important subject matter of the seven rays.

Almost all the other Bailey books included additional knowledge on the rays. Of particular interest and importance are *The Externalization of the Hierarchy, Treatise on White Magic, Letters on Occult Meditation, Glamour: A World Problem, Telepathy and the Etheric Vehicle, and Treatise on Cosmic Fire.*

**About the Arcane School.** The following paragraphs are quoted from the web site of the Lucis Trust—www.lucistrust.org.

"The Arcane School was established by Alice A. Bailey in 1923 to help meet an obvious and growing demand for further teaching and training in the science of the soul.

"The Arcane School was created as a training school for adult men and women in meditation techniques and the development of spiritual potentiality. The School provides sequential courses of study and meditation, and practical training in group service.

"The Arcane School is nonsectarian, and respects the right of each student to hold his/her own view and beliefs. It does not rely upon an authoritarian presentation of any one line of thought or code of ethics. Material used in the lesson courses is drawn from a variety of sources. The knowledge, insight and wisdom, and capacity to wield spiritual energy resulting from work and training with the Arcane School should be expressed and applied in daily living service in helping to materialise the Plan of God and to aid in solving the problems of humanity.

"The Arcane School is conducted by correspondence through headquarters in New York, London, and Geneva. The Arcane School is nonpolitical and nonsectarian. All are served. Since 1923 tens of thousands of students have taken advantage of the training.

"No charges are made by the School for its services. The work is financed through the Lucis Trust by the voluntary contributions of students and those interested in the work of the School and in the teaching. Each gives according to personal circumstances.

"The purpose of the esoteric training given in the Arcane School is to help the student grow spiritually toward acceptance of discipleship responsibility and to serve the Plan by serving humanity. Esotericism is a practical way of life."

Their address in the United States is: Lucis Trust,
                               120 Wall Street,
                               24th floor,
                               New York, NY 10005

In Great Britain: Lucis Trust
            suite 54
            3 Whitehall Court
            London, SW1A 2EF
            UK
And in Geneva: Lucis Trust
            1 rue de Varembe (3e)
            Case Postale 31
            1211 Geneva 20
            Switzerland

**Our Own Books and the**
**School for the Study of the Seven Rays**.............................

*Psychological Types and the Seven Rays*. This book explores primarily the three rays that generally condition the lower mental body—rays one, four, and five. This is done through a close look at how some prominent world figures thought.

The first ray mind we call the *administrative mind*. The examples we explore are Jane Addams and Mahatma Gandhi.

The fourth ray mind we call the *artistic-intuitive mind*. Examples discussed are Henry David Thoreau and Vincent van Gogh.

The fifth ray mind is the *scientific mind*. The examples we use to illustrate this mode of thought are Charles Darwin and Thomas Henry Huxley.

"By presenting a detailed evaluation of the personality, work, and life of real people, these distinct mental types come alive and support the use of ray analysis as a means to understand the whys and wherefores of human endeavors." E. James Faubel, in *Transformation Times*.

"Your book should be really useful to many. It establishes a precedent. I am honored to have the book dedicated to me." Mary Bailey, former President of the Lucis Trust.

*Threefold Method for Understanding the Seven Rays and Other Essays in Esoteric Psychology*. The lead essay discusses three sequential approaches to understanding the seven rays. The first stage has to do with the academic familiarization with the ray energies. This method employs primarily the intellect. At the same time, however, there is a gradual assimilation of ray knowledge that speaks to deeper levels of one's being.

The second stage has to do with a recognition of the group interplay of ray energies. The love of one's own type and ray is replaced by love of the which completes the whole. This moves more directly into the soul perspective. Several examples are given in order that one might see the livingness and the practicality of the ray energies.

The third stage has to be with becoming another ray. Sometimes circumstances forces developed people to move out of specialization and into "energies" and fields of work that are foreign to their own psychological ray make-up. Knowledge of this fascinating stage can help prepare one to recognize special opportunity. This third stage goes beyond soul and brings in a touch of spirit.

Other essays in the book include: "The Use of the Seven Rays in Dream Interpretation." "The Three Rays of Aspect and Stages of Development." This essay discusses the 3-2-1 sequence of first activity (growth through doing), then the deepening of conscious-ness, followed by maturity, power, and control. Seven year cycles and 21 year cycles are considered in this sequence.

"The Third Ray of Intelligent Activity Contrasted with Rays Four and Five." Subtle psychological differences between the approaches of these three rays are considered in some depth.

"First Ray: 'For You, There Must Be Not a Circle, But a Line.'" This essay considered the different approaches of the first ray and the second ray. The second ray type moves in a circle, looking at a broad base and comprehensive knowledge. The 1st ray type moves directly to the point of power in a straight line.

"Mr. Abraham's approach is pragmatic, using biographical information concerning prominent individuals to correlate an understanding of their life crises with an analysis of the Seven Ray make-up. His work will encourage further investigation into the nature and practical application of this most interesting field of study." *The Beacon*, published by the Lucis Trust.

"The Tibetan, throughout the Bailey books, exhorts us to study carefully the rays which are currently lacking in our equipment. To this end Abraham discusses several well-known personalities and how they coped, successfully or otherwise, with ray energies and qualities lacking in their makeup. These are brilliantly done and add much to our understanding of the rays and how they function in our lives.... This book helps loosen the girders of our concrete mind and widens the field of consciousness without neglecting to emphasize the important areas of work in the ray-fields." Rusi J. Daruwalla, in *Mandala, Esoteric Knowledge for the New Age*, published in Mumbai, India

***Techniques of Soul Alignment: The Rays, the Subtle Bodies, and the Use of KEYWORDS.*** This important psychological technique has to do with "avoiding the trap of many words"— a trap into which intellect and personality invariably fall—and using the *soul-to-soul single keyword technique.* This technique was used by D.K. in his work with his western students. It deals with a psychology of profound simplicity that leads to the revelation of one's higher spiritual possibilities.

There is always a subtle esoteric science behind the selection of a keyword. The keyword identifies and embodies a particular quality that is needed for balance and for soul unfoldment. This generally relates to the development or enhancement of a particular ray energy.

There is also a chapter dealing with four methods whereby one may discover one's own keywords.

***Balancing the Pairs of Opposites; The Seven Rays and Education; and Other Essays in Esoteric Psychology.***
From the text: "What does it mean to 'balance the pairs of opposites' and to 'walk the middle path'? How important a concept is this? Is it peripheral to the practicalities of daily life, or does it touch all aspects of our physical and psychological lives? Are there specific and practical techniques that can be used in the process of balancing the pairs of opposites?....

"It is important, it seems to me, to try to discuss this matter as concretely as possible, for the subject matter itself is primarily a

128

psychological process or relative abstraction. Also it seems to me that if the interplay of opposites is 'at once the most individual fact and the most universal,' then there is also a most practical application of this 'union' or relationship in nearly every human situation and at most every developmental level. Alice Bailey attests to the comprehensiveness of this process in the following statements: 'The interplay of the opposites . . . is the underlying theme of the entire creative and evolutionary process.' 'Through the interplay of the poles, and through the friction of the pairs of opposites light flashes forth. The goal of evolution is found to be a gradual series of light demonstrations." (*Esoteric Astrology* 391, *Treatise on White Magic* 9.)"

"A reading of Mr. Abraham's book *Balancing the Pairs of Opposites* makes one whisper 'Here's richness.'...This book is to be read several times; only then can one gain from the immense insights so casually granted by Kurt Abraham in paragraph after paragraph." Rusi J. Daruwalla, in *Mandala, Esoteric Knowledge for the New Age*, published in Mumbai, India.

The essay on the "Seven Rays and Education" includes:
Determining the Child's Note and Quality.
The Rays and Stages of Development.
Feeling Beauty, Strength, and Wisdom—Differences in Learning
    Approaches Between Children and Adults.
The Feeling Approach.
The Rays and the Emotional Plane.
The Mental Approach. The Ray of Mind.
The Higher Self or Soul. Meaning, Quality, Value.
Love, Patience, Understanding, and Ordered Activity.
The Science of Service. Future Schools.
A Transition Period. The Time Factor.
    Other essays in the book include:
"The Seven Rays in Literature:" King Arthur—First Ray Type.
King Lear and a second ray Glamour. A Character Drawing in Legend of Sleepy Hollow.
"Carl Rogers and His Most Prominent Rays."
"The Ray of the Elephant."

***The Moon Veils Vulcan and the Sun Veils Neptune***.  This book explores the enigmatic statement in Esoteric Astrology: "The Moon is usually regarded as 'veiling' or 'hiding' some planet and of these there are three which the Moon may be veiling.  Here the intuition of the astrologer and of the esoteric student must be called out.   These planets are Vulcan, Neptune or Uranus....  Instead of working with the Moon, let astrologers work with Vulcan when dealing with the undeveloped or average man and with Uranus when considering the highly developed man....  If the investigating astrologer will study the 'fluid area' where the planets, veiled by the Sun and Moon, come into play and will realize that he must decide what is the point in evolution reached and which of the three veiled planets is the ruler, he will get much intuitive understanding."

***The Seven Rays and Nations: France and the United States Compared***.  Sub-headings of the essay on France and the US are:

The Intellectual Plays a Prominent Role in France.
Rhetorical Tricks of Staggering Ingenuity.
Lack of Practicality.
A 'Bogus Politeness' Resulting in 'Suspiciousness.'
The 2nd and the 6th Rays in American Companies.
An Experience in France.
Attraction or Repulsion to a Foreign Culture
    due to One's Own Individual Rays.
The Leo Influence and the French Personality.
The Leo Personality and the Third Ray.
The U.S.'s Noninterference by Government compared
    to France's Complex Bureaucracies.
The Soul of France.
French and American Films Contrasted as they
    Present Characteristics of the National Rays.
The French and American People Contrasted.
The Difficulty of Seeing Oneself or the Rays of
    One's Own Nation.

"I was extremely impressed by your book on the Rays and Nations. Your comparisons of France and the united States was especially insightful. I also thought that your applications to business were extremely practical. This is an area that I have been working in for a number of years. I have incorporated many of your ideas in the workshops that I give for business people."

John Cullen, President of International Association for Managerial and Organizational Psychosynthesis.

**Book Ordering Information.** We welcome orders direct to the publisher. For ordering information, including prices and our latest books please write to:

LAMPUS PRESS
19611 ANTIOCH ROAD
WHITE CITY, OREGON 97503

**The School for the Study of the Seven Rays.**

The School for the Study of the Seven Rays (SS7R) offers a Home Study Course that is approximately 2 years in length with additional material for advanced studies. No fees are charged. The School is supported entirely by contributions from the students. Extensive individual attention is given to the work of each student. Sample Newsletters are available on request.

"Pioneers" are sorely needed in this slow but steady work of bringing in a more meaningful psychology—a psychology that addresses the spiritual/soul aspects of being (as well as the threefold personality), and also a psychology that greatly enhances one's ability to be of service to others.

For further information please write:

SS7R
19611 ANTIOCH ROAD
WHITE CITY, OR 97503
U.S.A.

# BIBLIOGRAPHY

Abraham, Kurt. *Psychological Types and the Seven Rays.* White
  City, Oregon: Lampus Press, 1983.

—————— *Threefold Method for Understanding the Seven Rays and
  Other Essays in Esoteric Psychology.* White City,
  Oregon: Lampus Press, 1984.

Bailey, Alice A. *A Compilation on Sex.* New York: Lucis
  Publishing Co.

—————— *Destiny of Nations.* New York: Lucis Publishing Co.,
  1949.

—————— *Discipleship in the New Age.* New York: Lucis
  Publishing Co., 1944.

—————— *Education in the New Age.* New York: Lucis Publishing
  Co., 1954.

——————*Esoteric Astrology.* New York: Lucis Publishing Co.

—————— *Esoteric Healing.* New York: Lucis Publishing Co.,
  1953.

—————— *Externalization of the Hierarchy.* New York: Lucis
  Publishing Co., 1957.

—————— *Problems of Humanity.* New York: Lucis Publishing.

—————— *Telepathy and the Etheric Vehicle.* New York: Lucis
  Publishing Co.,

—————— *Treatise on Cosmic Fire.* New York: Lucis Publishing
  Co., 1925.

—————— *Treatise on White Magic.* New York, Lucis Publishing
  Co., 1934.

Caddy, Peter. *In Perfect Timing.* Forres, Scotland: Findhorn
  Press, 1996.

DeVille, Dr. Jard. *The Psychology of Leadership.* New York:
  Farnswoth Publishing Co., 1984.

Hock, Dee. *Birth of the Chaordic Age.* San Francisco:
  Barrett-Koehler Publishers, Inc., 1999.

Mananovic, Milenko. "Interview with James Parks Morton, Dean
  of Cathedral of St. John the Divine, New York." *Lorian
  Journal* (Vol. III, No. 1).

Steiner, Rudolf. *Conferences with Teachers*. New York: Anthroposophical Press, 1921.
——— *Esoteric Development*. New York: Anthroposophical Press, 1982.
——— *The Cycle of the Year*. New York: Anthroposophical Press, 1923.
——— *The Influences of Lucifer and Ahriman*. New York: Anthroposophical Press.
——— *The Social Future*. New York: Anthroposophical Press, 1945.
——— *Towards Social Renewal: Basic Issues of the Social Question*. Bristol, Great Britain: Rudolf Steiner Press, 1992.

Wright, Robin. *The Last Great Revolution: Turmoil and Transformation in Iran*. New York: Knopf, 2000.

# INDEX